Coaching for Engagement

Achieving Results Through Powerful Conversations

By: Bob Hancox, Russell Hunter & Kristann Boudreau

ORGANIZATIONAL EFFECTIVENESS INC.

ORGANIZATIONAL EFFECTIVENESS INC.

405-808 Nelson Street

Vancouver, BC CANADA

V6Z 2H2

For information about special discounts for bulk purchases of this book, please contact Tekara at 1.888.883.5272 or info@tekara.com

Tekara can bring one of the authors to speak at your live event. For more information or to book a speaker, please contact Tekara at 1.888.883.5272 or visit: www.coachingforengagement.com

Manufactured in the United States of America

10   9   8   7   6   5   4   3   2   1

ISBN 978-0-9867005-0-7

To our clients,
who continually inspire us to come up with innovative and effective ways
to help them face the challenges of leadership in today's workplace.

Table of Contents

PART IV: TAKING ACTION: BRIDGING THE GAP FROM KNOWING TO DOING

The chief responsibility of a manager:
to turn one person's talent into performance.

- Marcus Buckingham

Introduction

This book is for busy managers who are looking for more effective ways to get work done through their people. It's for managers who need and want to help improve their direct reports' performance and ability to generate business results. It's for managers who want to help their people stay engaged, focused and productive. It's for managers who realize that they spend most of their day communicating and want to create conversations that have a bigger impact.

The line of thought that inspired us to write this book goes something like this: the managers we work with all want to improve their ability to contribute to their organizations. What do their organizations want from them? *Bottom-line results.* What generates those results? Sustained high performance from their people. What drives that kind of performance? High levels of individual and team engagement. What drives engagement? Many factors, and one of the strongest connecting threads among them is the quality of relationships that managers build with their employees and teams, and the effectiveness and impact of the conversations they have. What could help managers strengthen relationships and have more effective conversations? Adopting a coaching style. Sounds logical. So what's the problem?

Most organizations take on more than they can handle. This leaves managers deluged with accelerated action plans, higher performance goals, shortened innovation cycles, and the simultaneous introduction of new or revised organizational systems. As a result, most managers are so busy focusing on their own work and whatever is most urgent, they have no time left over to focus on developing and coaching their people. Instead, they "manage by exception," only dealing with problems, mistakes, and complaints about their employees. To sum up the problem most managers are facing: *"Too much work to do, no time to coach."*

As understandable as this pattern is, unfortunately, it can have costly consequences. When managers focus only on results or on what's not working, then employees disengage: they either quit and leave, or worse, quit and stay. Either way, those employees stop helping to achieve the very results that managers are chasing.

Given that the enormous time and performance pressure we all face is not going away, what's a manager to do? Make the most of the time available. The less time employees have with their manager, the more positive and meaningful that time needs to be – the more each conversation needs to count.

Coaching conversations are designed to help both managers and their people get more out of the conversation. By adopting a *coaching* stance rather than a *directive* one, managers get relief from the exhaustive and never-ending task of solving other's problems and telling them what to do next. Using coaching, managers launch a positive spiral that invites more initiative, more productivity, and greater effectiveness from employees over time.

As a participant in coaching conversations, employees get a welcome opportunity to be supported in clarifying their thinking, proposing new ideas, providing valuable insights and perspectives, developing their problem-solving abilities, mapping next steps, and shaping their role and contribution – all of which increase their level of engagement. Coaching conversations make each conversation count – for the manager, for the employee, and for the organization.

Here is how one manager describes the difference it makes taking a coaching approach with staff rather than just directing like a boss:

About four years ago I began working with an executive coach who had been very helpful in assisting me to gain increasing self-awareness about how I interact with my leadership team. At that time, [we] began to discuss new ways of interacting, including asking questions rather than telling. I had always been inclined to offer solutions rather than empower people to solve their own problems. I just automatically assumed that if someone was at my door with a problem, they expected me to solve it ... I realized how disempowering this is, and how much more effective I could be by posing the question back to the individual with the problem. This took active concentration on my part to practice this new behaviour ... What I came to realize is that solving others' problems is exhausting. It is much more effective to provide the opportunity for them to solve their own problems. So instead of jumping in with a quick response when someone would come to me, I began responding this way: 'Well, I am sure you have had time to think about this and have your own ideas, what have you come up with?' This type of question is very validating, and lets the person know that I respect their knowledge and experience. I have come to believe that solving people's problems sends a message that you don't think they can do it themselves. Very often people have thought out their answers and just want to test them with someone else. I now give them a chance to do that.[1]

In this book, we advocate that coaching is an extremely effective but underutilized approach managers can use to increase employee engagement, which in turn, generates enhanced performance and business results. Our goal is to encourage you and equip you to join the many managers with whom we've worked to starting using coaching conversations as a powerful tool for increasing engagement in your workplace. We also want to encourage you to use coaching skills to improve the quality and impact of your interactions with others in your workplace, including colleagues and even your boss.

How the Book Is Organized

This book is divided into four parts. In Part I, we explore the various reasons that it makes sense for managers to build coaching skills and adopt a coaching style of management. How can conversations drive the kind of engagement that yields high performance and results? What is coaching? What are the "push factors" or workplace trends that are driving the need for more manager-coaches? What are the "pull factors" that make coaching a win for you as a manager? How do we dispel some key myths about coaching as a manager? What are the key challenges of being a manager-coach? How does trust play into it? These are the questions we address in Chapters one and two.

Part II is devoted to walking you through a set of fundamental coaching skills. Chapter 3 introduces you to our Coaching Conversations Trailmap, including our C.O.A.C.H. approach: Curious Questioning, Open Listening, Appreciative Discovery, Catalytic Feedback, Heightened Engagement. Before focusing on each of these skills in more detail, we devote our attention in Chapter 4 to the four key mindset shifts we need to be effective as coaches: from treating colleagues as lacking and inadequate, to treating them as creative, resourceful and capable; from assuming that you already know, to listening for what your colleagues know; from telling people what to do, to asking people how they want to contribute; from trying to understand the underlying cause of a problem, to trying to solve the problem. In Chapters 5 through 10, we focus on one coaching skill at a time.

Part III is devoted to providing you with some very practical advice and tools you can start using immediately. Chapter 11 explores how you can prepare yourself and your employees for a successful coaching experience. Chapter 12 walks you through how to prepare for an upcoming coaching conversation: choosing the timing and setting, making the shift into a coaching mindset, using the "Ask-Tell" conversation planning tool, and preparing yourself mentally and emotionally as you head into the conversation. Chapter 13 provides you with sample scripts (sequences of coaching questions) for walking through some of the most common types of coaching conversations you will encounter as a manager.

Finally, in Part IV we focus on implementation: how great managers begin implementing these new skills on a daily basis. Chapter 14 introduces you to a four-step development process used by high performers to accelerate your growth and development as a manager-coach. This process will help you move rapidly from knowing to doing, from reading and learning about key coaching skills to actually using them on a daily basis.

We conclude the book with a short perspective on the positive ripple effect of managers adopting a coaching style.

A Note on Language

In the early part of the book, we'll introduce the term "coachee" which refers to whomever you're coaching in a particular conversation. Throughout most of the book, however, we've opted to use the word employee, for a couple of reasons. The first is that "coachee" is an awkward word. The second is that in all likelihood, most of the time you will be using your coaching skills with employees. Please keep in mind, though, that coaching skills can be used to increase the impact and productivity of conversations with almost anyone in your workplace, including colleagues, your own boss and other senior leaders.

You'll also see us refer to the "manager-coach." This label recognizes that when managers are coaching they are wearing two hats. The first is their manager hat, which keeps them focused on harnessing employees' performance to achieve organizational results in the short-term. The second is their coaching hat, which encourages them to focus on the employee's long-term development.

What We Hope You Will Take Away From This Book

When we set out to write this book, we hoped to impart two key insights, and some helpful skills and tools. When it comes to insight, here are the two key messages we want to leave with you:

- Coaching is not simply a technique for dealing with performance issues. It is a powerful business practice that can increase results by increasing engagement.

- Coaching is first and foremost a mindset, not just a set of tools and techniques.

In terms of skills and tools, we want to equip you with:

- A set of six integrated, foundational coaching conversations skills.

- A set of practical tools for having coaching conversations, from preparing ahead of time, to walking through the conversation, to closing and following up.

- A simple action plan outlining how you'll start weaving coaching conversations into your everyday interactions and build your confidence along the way – based on proven principles of skill development. Learning how to coach, like practicing any new skill, is much easier if we harness the fundamentals of behavioural change.

With awareness comes the opportunity to make new choices. Read on and we'll show you how choosing to have coaching conversations can help you achieve greater results with your employees. Over the course of the book, we'll equip you with the practical skills and tools you need to follow through successfully on that choice.

PART I: COACHING AS A MANAGER

"The most valuable source of high performance and competitive advantage is a workforce that consistently performs at its best. But employees do this only if they're engaged in their work."

- Julie Gebauer and Don Lowman

Chapter 1

From Manager to Manager-Coach – Why Make the Shift?

In this chapter, we'll focus on helping you decide that coaching is something you'd like to add to your repertoire as a manager. We'll discuss:

- why increasing the impact of your conversations is critical to your success as a manager, allowing you to cultivate higher performance and sustained business results

- how coaching is both an activity/skill and a style of management

- how a coaching style of management compares to other styles

- the "push factors" (workplace trends) and "pull factors" (benefits for you as a manager) driving the increasing use of a coaching style of management.

- If you're already convinced of the value of coaching as a manager, by all means, skip to the next chapter where we'll dispel some common myths, address the inherent challenges of coaching as a manager, and discuss the crucial role trust plays in successful coaching.

- If you're also interested in learning more about the organizational business case for investing in building managers' coaching conversation skills, please download a copy from the book website at: *www.coachingforengagement.com*

Conversations Drive Engagement, Performance & Results

We developed the Tekara Results Peak™ (Figure 1) to better illustrate and interpret the connection and links between conversations and bottom-line results. It takes a strong foundation to reach the peak, so we'll start at the bottom and work our way to the top.

Figure 1: Tekara Results Peak™

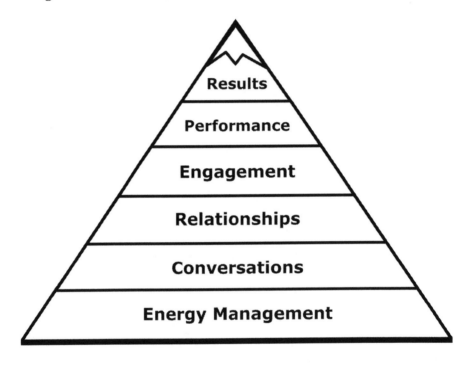

The path to results begins with what we call personal *energy management* – each of us being aware of our levels of physical, emotional and mental energy and devoting them to advancing our team's and organization's mission (we talk more about this in Chapter 5). When we are managing our own energy well, we can have respectful and constructive and authentic *conversations* with each other. Over time, those conversations translate into good *relationships* – between managers and employees, within teams, between teams and between all levels of the organization. Together, these three things – people managing their energy well, having productive conversations, and building relationships – drive **engagement**. When individuals and teams are fully engaged – when they are motivated, committed and giving a project or ongoing program their best – then high **performance** often occurs. Sustaining high levels of individual and team performance is what ultimately leads to top-line and bottom-line **results**.

As a manager, your employees' level of performance and the results they achieve are likely your biggest concerns. Having worked with hundreds of managers over the years, our experience tells us that the most effective way to drive higher employee performance is actually to focus one layer down on the Results Peak, on engagement.

When employees are engaged, they bring something extra to their work: a discretionary level of effort, creativity and commitment that goes beyond the minimum acceptable contribution. They harness their skills, talents and experience to deliver high quality work that moves the organization forward. If you help your employees increase their level of engagement, you won't have to rely as heavily on the carrots and sticks of performance management to motivate and manage them.[2] To build engagement, your strongest sphere of influence is the realm of conversations and relationships. That's where coaching fits in.

What Is Coaching?

Coaching can be simply a stand-alone activity, or a style of management. As an activity in the work context, *coaching is a way of focusing and leading a conversation* with the intent of facilitating learning, heightening engagement, and encouraging higher performance. What goes on during a coaching conversation that makes it different from most workplace conversations? The focus of the "coach" (manager) is on the thinking process of the "coachee" (employee), while the focus of the "coachee" (employee) is on the issue (problem or opportunity) they bring to the table, as illustrated in the diagram below (Figure 2). By contrast, in most conversations at work, both people are focusing on the issue on the table, with the employee expecting the manager to solve the problem, or find the solution for them. In essence, when you are coaching, you are helping people get better at thinking their way through problems, opportunities and make decisions themselves.

Figure 2: Roles During a Coaching Conversation[3]

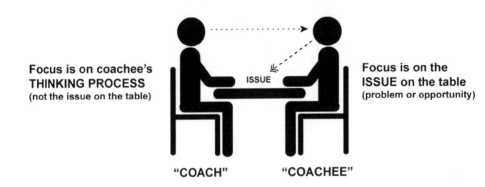

Focus is on coachee's
THINKING PROCESS
(not the issue on the table)

ISSUE

Focus is on the
ISSUE on the table
(problem or opportunity)

"COACH"   **"COACHEE"**

As an activity, coaching also shows up as a set of skills the manager-coach uses during the conversation: asking powerful questions, listening intently, discovering and appreciating strengths, and giving effective feedback. We talk about these more in Chapters 5 through 10. What's less obvious on the surface – but critical to a manager's success in building and using coaching skills – are the shifts in mindset that a manager-coach makes:

- from treating people as lacking and inadequate, to treating them as creative, resourceful and capable

- from assuming that you already know, to listening to what others know

- from telling people what to do, to asking people how they want to contribute

- from trying to understand the underlying cause of a problem, to trying to solve the problem.

We talk about these mindset shifts in more detail in Chapter 4.

Adopting coaching as a management style goes beyond building coaching skills and shifting your mindset during certain conversations. It also means:

- being more collaborative

- delegating more responsibility

- asking for more input and acting on it

- giving less advice, letting go of needing to have all the answers, and helping others develop their own solutions

- balancing your need for short-term employee performance and results from their long-term need for growth and development.

We are not suggesting that coaching is the only style you should use (i.e., you need to make a complete switch and use this style all the time, in all situations). There are many styles of leadership, and each one has a time and a place (see Table 1). The most successful managers often have a combination of three or four different styles they use in the course of a week, depending on the situation. Emotional intelligence specialist Daniel Goleman and two of his colleagues identified six styles of leadership[4] that are used to varying degrees in today's workplace: Commanding, Pacesetting, Visionary, Affiliative, Democratic, and Coaching (see Table 1). They have also identified the situations in which each style can be most helpful and effective.

Table 1: Styles of Leadership[5]

	Commanding	Pacesetting	Visionary	Affiliative	Democratic	Coaching
Goal	Give clear direction	Set challenging and exciting goals (and standards for performance)	Mobilize people toward a shared vision	Create harmony and connect people	Build commitment through participation	Connect an employee's goals with the organization's goals
Situations when the style works best	In a crisis To kick start a turnaround With problem employees	To get quick, high-quality results from a highly motivated and competent team	When changes require a new vision, or when a clear direction is needed	To heal rifts in a team To motivate people during stressful times	To build buy-in or consensus To gather valuable input from employees	To help an employee improve performance by building long-term capabilities

This is where the distinction we made earlier – between coaching as an activity (or set of skills) and as a style of management – becomes important. While only one of the styles is explicitly labeled as "Coaching," the skills you will learn in this book can enhance your effectiveness in using three of the other styles as well: Visionary, Affiliative, and Democratic.

We encourage you to consider adopting a coaching style with your employees wherever possible (we'll talk later in this chapter about when it might be more or less appropriate), and to use your coaching skills to enhance your management.

Why Invest in Learning to Coach as a Manager?

It's not hard to see how coaching benefits an employee or any colleague you might coach; we all welcome help thinking through a tough situation. But what about you – what's in it for you as a manager? Why invest the time and energy in learning to coach as a manager when there are already so many demands on you? Will your investment pay off?

In this section we talk about a number of "push factors," or reasons you can't afford not to invest in learning to coach, as well as the strong "pull factors" or reasons you'll be glad you made the time to acquire coaching skills.

"Push Factors": Workplace Trends You Can't Ignore

Consider two workplace trends that are becoming difficult to sidestep; ignoring them is costly. The first is the growing "engagement gap," the second is the increasing demand for more collaborative styles of management.

1. **Growing engagement gap.** We all like to think that disengaged employees are in the minority in our organizations. Maybe you've got a team and workplace that beats the odds, but here are some sobering statistics from two leading employee engagement researchers.[6] Most organizations, departments and teams are operating at 1/5 to 1/4 of

their people potential. That means that on your team, for every person that is fully engaged, there are 3 or 4 or who have more to offer. That's a big "engagement gap" – and productivity gap. It's also an opportunity: imagine what you could accomplish if your entire team were operating at full steam. Coaching can help you close the engagement gap on your team and start to generate higher performance and productivity.

2. **Growing preference for a coaching style of management**. One of the key factors driving employee engagement is the quality of their relationship with their immediate supervisor/manager. Marcus Buckingham (formerly with The Gallup Organization), once noted that people join organizations but leave managers. If you've lost an employee and been through a hiring process recently, you know the impact it has on your productivity and on that of your team. Coaching will help you become a manager with committed employees, because coaching provides employees with more of what they're looking for.

   In today's workplace, employees respond more to supportive and coach-like styles of management – and less to coercive and authoritarian styles. If you flip back to the table earlier in this chapter where we compared and contrasted leadership styles, this means that employees' preference is increasingly for Visionary, Affiliative, Democratic and Coaching styles. While this is true across all generations in the workforce, it is particularly true of Generation Y employees (Millenials). Recent research has found that Millenials rate "working with a manager I respect and can learn from" as the most important factor in their work environment.[7] More specifically, they are looking to their manager for: frequent communication, frequent feedback on their performance (including practical suggestions for improvement), trust in their ability to get the job done, and opportunities to discuss and plan for their professional growth and development. A coaching style of management is the most likely to meet these needs.

These are the key factors pushing you towards investing in becoming a manager-coach. Now, the question is: what's in it for you? What are the wins you can expect as a manager in return for your investment?

"Pull Factors": The Win for You as a Manager

Here are just a few of the benefits that we've seen managers experience as they begin to adopt a more coach-like style and use the skills in this book:

1. **Better working relationships.** Good coaching requires that the employee trust the manager's commitment to their success, and that the manager trust in the employee's ability to get the job done. As trust builds, your working relationships become more enjoyable (or in some cases, at least less stressful).

2. **Better and more creative ideas.** Coaching has a way of starting a positive spiral when it comes to creativity. When you get into the habit of asking questions to draw out people's creativity, you may be pleasantly surprised at what people come up with – and how they start bringing you helpful suggestions without you even having to ask.

3. **Fewer monkeys on your back.** One of our Associates at Tekara, Leona Kolla, describes a very vivid illustration of this that still sticks in her mind. An instructor in a leadership program she attended demonstrated what it looks like when a manager takes on other people's problems (monkeys). The instructor had plush toy monkeys (with Velcro paws) all over him – on his back, arms, head, torso and legs. Through coaching conversations, he gradually pulled each monkey off and began putting them on other people, giving back the monkeys (problems) to the people they belonged to. By taking a coaching approach, you can help people work through their own challenges, rather than having to take them all on yourself. You've got enough other responsibilities on your plate!

4. **Less work for you as employees take more initiative.** When you coach someone to set their own goals, make decisions and implement their own ideas, they are far more likely to feel committed and to follow through. But more importantly, having been guided through the process once by you, they start to develop the "thinking muscles" that will allow them to do it again on their own. Over time, their confidence and competence increase, and they are much more likely to take more

initiative – meaning less work for you in the long run. That leaves you free to focus on the more strategic and enjoyable parts of your own job.

5. **Opportunity to invest in others and contribute to their growth and development.** Clearly this is a longer-term win or benefit – but it's an important one to mention. Leaving a legacy of growth and development is both about the way you want to be remembered, and the ripple effect you want to have created in people's lives. If you think about the leaders, managers and mentors who have had a positive impact on your life and career, it's likely they had many of the qualities and skills of a good coach. They took an interest in you, they were committed to your success, and they probably took the time to ask you powerful questions and listen openly. When you coach your employees, you can feel proud knowing that you are carrying on this legacy, contributing to their growth and development.

We hope that by this point, you're feeling motivated to dive into learning about the specific skills you need to have effective coaching conversations. Before we walk you through the core tools in Part II of the book, we've dedicated the next chapter to clarifying what's involved in coaching as a manager. We'll dispel some common myths, address the two inherent challenges of coaching as a manager, and emphasize the crucial role trust plays in successful coaching.

What to Take Away from This Chapter

*   To drive high performance and results, managers need to focus on heightening employee engagement. One of the most effective ways to do that is through coaching.

*   Coaching is both a stand-alone activity (a way of focusing and leading a conversation) and a management style (that focuses on growth and development).

*   The main difference between a coaching conversation and a typical workplace conversation is that the focus of the coach (manager) is on the

thinking process of the "coachee" (employee), while the focus of the employee is on the issue (problem or opportunity) they are facing.

- At its core, coaching is about helping people get better at thinking their way through problems, opportunities and decisions.

- Coaching is one of many styles of management; each has its time and place. Successful managers often have a combination of three or four different styles they draw on depending on the situation.

- The workplace trends acting as "push factors" urging you to build your coaching skills include: a growing disengagement among employees, and a shifting preference among employees for a coaching style of management.

- The "pull factors" or benefits for you of adopting a coaching approach as a manager include: better working relationships, better and more creative ideas from your employees, less ownership of other people's problems, less work for you as your employees take more initiative, and the satisfaction of knowing you are creating a legacy of growth and development.

*"The most basic principle for becoming a manager-coach [is]
creating an open and safe relationship with employees so they can begin to see
their mistakes, admit their weaknesses, and talk about their potential,
that is, so far, just potential."*

- David Logan and John King

Chapter 2

Coaching as a Manager: Myths, Challenges and Building Trust

What are you getting yourself into if you decide to be a manager-coach? In this chapter we'll discuss:

- the most common myths about coaching as a manager

- the inherent challenges shared by all manager-coaches

- the importance of building trust in order to coach successfully.

The key message we hope you take away from his chapter is that while coaching is a departure from traditional management and will require effort on your part, the results make it worthwhile and there are ways to ease the transition.

Dispelling Myths About Coaching as a Manager

Here are the most common myths we run into when we work with managers who are contemplating adopting a coaching approach.

- **Myth #1 – Leading means having all the answers and telling people what to do: if you're coaching, you're not leading**. As managers, most of us receive years and years of training in being forceful, articulate advocates. Along the way we are praised for our ability to solve problems, answer every question, and give timely advice to others. That's why coaching – and particularly the initial step of asking more questions – can feel uncomfortable at first. And it's not just you thinking you need to have all the answers – your employees are trained to believe it too. Only recently have we started to see a shift in the role of leaders – from being charismatic decision-makers and infallible bosses to becoming people who facilitate questioning and problem solving. So while trying on the "coaching hat" may feel uncomfortable for you at first, it will also feel different for your employees when they see you taking a different approach – helping them think through problems rather than doing the thinking for them.

So why coach if people just want an answer from you? Well, they do and they don't. People do want to get unstuck, or generate the results that are eluding them. But they don't necessarily need to have the answer come from you. The best part about coaching is that when it's successful, it generates results (an "answer") <u>and</u> deeper learning.

Giving advice may generate short term results, but it can rob the people we lead of deeper learning and development. By getting caught in the trap of constantly giving advice or trying to solve the problem, you can perpetuate a cycle that doesn't develop capacity of your team – not to mention consume more of your time and energy than is necessary. When you help an employee find the answer themselves, they build their self-awareness, creativity, resourcefulness and competence. Deeper learning takes place when ownership of a solution comes from the employee.

- **Myth #2 – Only certain people should coach as managers**. Some managers worry they don't have the right personality or work style to coach effectively. In our experience, that fear is unfounded. The managers we've worked with have all found a way to use the coaching conversation skills that feel natural for them. Any awkwardness they might experience at first is simply what we all experience when we're practicing a new skill – not a sign they are somehow innately unsuited to coaching.

A related but unfounded myth is that coaching only works in certain workplace cultures. As we've introduced Coaching for Engagement™ to multinational organizations in India and China, we've discovered that coaching conversations have just as positive an effect there as in North America. However, each culture does seem to find that different aspects of coaching (e.g., certain mindsets or skills) come more naturally to them while others are more challenging for them.

- **Myth #3 – Coaching is too time-consuming.** It's true that coaching does require an up-front investment of your time in order to gain time in the long-run. It's true that it probably will be faster for you to take charge and give advice or order instead of coaching – but only in the short-term. But the more you direct, the more people will rely on you for direction, until you find large chunks of your time being swallowed up by their over-reliance. Think of coaching as the road to successful delegation. By investing time in coaching you are helping people to become more capable and self-reliant, needing less and less direction from you. Then you get to reap the benefit of all the time you've now freed up to focus on the tasks only you can accomplish.

  One other perspective to take on coaching as a wise investment of time relates to employee retention. Employees who are less engaged are far more likely to leave an organization. Spending a little bit of extra time coaching for engagement – and reaping the benefits of enhanced performance and results – is a far more productive (and more pleasant) use of your time than recruiting and training a new employee.

- **Myth #4 – Coaching conversations are just pleasant, warm and fuzzy.** Coaching isn't just about having "nicer" interactions; it also involves maintaining a strong focus on goals and results. We certainly encourage manager-coaches to discover, appreciate and affirm their employees' strengths and to "cheerlead" now and then. However, when questions become sharper and deeper, the value of coaching surfaces, helping employees get to the next layer in their thinking. This is not about asking interrogative, drilling or judgmental questions, but rather gently challenging with powerful, curious questions that will move them toward greater insight, and ultimately, into committed action. For example: *What are the next steps you know you need to take? What's holding you back? What needs to be handled for you to move forward?*

- **Myth #5 – If you've received coaching yourself, then you inherently know how to use coaching skills with other people.** It's tempting to think this way – if only it were that easy, and you could learn the skills by osmosis! Our experience with our clients tells us that being coached yourself certainly does help you develop your coaching skills: it gives you an example of good coaching to emulate, and helps you understand what it's like to be sitting in the chair of the "coachee." Unfortunately, there is no substitute for learning coaching skills the way we learn anything: through practice.

Next, we take a look at some of the special dynamics facing a manager-coach.

Inherent Challenges Shared by All Manager-Coaches

There are two key challenges that come with the territory of coaching as a manager (i.e., coaching direct reports). The first is wearing two hats: balancing your agenda as a manager (focusing on performance), and your agenda as a coach (focusing on helping employees exercise choice, grow, and find purpose in their work). The second is learning to discern when to use a coaching style (and when not to). Both challenges are definitely surmountable with a bit of awareness and forethought.

Balancing Two Agendas: Performance & Development

One question we often get from participants in our Coaching for Engagement™ program is: *"These skills are great, but how do I have coaching conversations knowing that I'm under pressure to get results?"* The underlying challenge they're voicing is partly about time pressure, but also about balancing agendas: the performance- and results-oriented agenda of a manager, and the learning and development agenda of a coach. As a manager interacting with employees, your primary focus is on your need for them to perform well and produce results that support organizational goals – this quarter. As a coach, you want to support your employees' long-term development and their pursuit of increased input, influence, choice, learning, growth and purpose in their work. As a manager-coach, you need to find a way to balance both agendas.

Our suggestion for handling this is to lead with your coaching hat, and follow-up with your manager hat, using questions to help your employees keep this balance in mind. It's a matter of staying open to the possibility that you can find an overlap between both agendas: maintaining a "both/and" perspective, rather than falling into the "either/or" thinking trap. For example: "I see you'd like to attend such-and-such conference/event. What excites/interests you about it in terms of your own learning (coach agenda)? I can really hear your enthusiasm when you talk about it. Now, help me understand how this will help you improve in your role (manager agenda)? How can we make sure you get a chance to apply what you learn? What kind of knowledge, tools or skills do you think you'll bring back – and how will you apply them to one of your current projects?"

Or perhaps you've been having conversations with one of your employees for some time about their particular strengths and their career goals. Maybe it's becoming obvious they're not in the best role given those strengths and goals. But for now, they're still a member of your team. What do you do? You might ask questions like: *"What kind of work really energizes you? How could you adjust the role you're playing on one of your current projects (manager agenda) so that you get to do more interesting work and use your strengths more often (coach agenda)? If you could create a brand new role for yourself on this team, what would you like to do (coach agenda) that would help us achieve our team's goals and targets (manager agenda)? While we probably can't create that position for you right now, what ideas does this give you for the meantime?"*

You get the picture. Look for the opportunities to advance both agenda, to achieve both performance and development.

Knowing When to Use a Coaching Style of Management

Here are some simple guidelines to help you navigate the decision of when to use a coaching style (see Table 2). By offering you these guidelines, we hope to save you the frustration of applying coaching in situations where it is not well suited, and when it is unlikely to be helpful or successful.

Table 2: When to Use a Coaching Style[8]

When Coaching Can Be Helpful: Conditions that Need to Be In Place for Successful Coaching	What You Can Try If Those Coaching Conditions Are Not In Place
Employee has the skills and ability to complete the task at hand, but for some reason is struggling with an internal block: confidence, focus, motivation, drive	If the employee needs to develop specific skills and abilities to complete the task, then either provide them with detailed instruction yourself and supervise them closely while they try it the first time, or find them training.
Employee has the skills and ability to complete the task at hand, but is facing external factors impeding success (such as a lack of available resources, changing market conditions, interpersonal challenges, lack of support or sponsorship). For coaching to work, the employee must already have the skills and abilities to deal with these external factors.	If the employee has the skills and ability to complete the task – but not to deal with the external factors impeding their success – then you may need to either give them advice or intervene yourself on their behalf if that's appropriate.
Employee is "coachable" or open to being coached (they want help, they want to get unstuck, they are motivated to improve).	Most employees are "coachable"(particularly if you are a skilled, patient and persistent coach). But there are a few exceptions you should be aware of: - Truly arrogant and intimidating employees who don't realize they are arrogant or the impact they have on others. These are different than employees who are generally overconfident but who will admit some fault or responsibility under the right circumstances. Our advice: avoid trying to coach these folks when you are first building your skills. - Employees who do not appear interested in learning. One of the most likely reasons for this is that they are either not suited to their job, or don't like it. You can use coaching questions to explore this topic. Depending on what you learn, it may be that the best outcome is for you to help the employee remove themselves from the organization in a positive way.

	- Employees under significant personal stress. We all have the ability to handle and juggle a variety of stressors in our life, but we also have a threshold where the load becomes too great. If your employee has reached that tipping point, seek out focused support for them from someone knowledgeable in this area; for example, a representative of your organization's employee assistance program. Discuss with your employee what you can do to support them during this time (relieving them of a high-stress project, moving to part-time status, taking time off, etc.).
Employee is open to being coached <u>by you.</u>	If they are open to being coached – but not by you (perhaps because they are struggling in their working relationship with you) – then consider helping them find another internal coach in your organization, or an outside coach.
You are not in the midst of a crisis or emergency.	If the circumstances are dire and time is of the essence, then what is really called for is a more directive style of management: tell people what to do.

Please note: while we spent time in the guidelines outlined in Table 2 exploring a few categories of employees who may be less coachable at a particular time in their career, in our experience, they are rare. A lack of coachability is the exception rather than the norm. It is far more likely that all of the employees on your team are coachable, but how you approach the coaching conversation may need to be adjusted to suit each one.

On a related note, there's been an evolution in thinking about when to take a coaching approach depending on an employee's existing level of performance and engagement. At first, it was something to do in remedial situations, to address performance problems and to "deal with" actively disengaged employees. Unfortunately, this has coloured some people's impression of coaching, believing that it is only for "wimps" or "problem" employees.

Thankfully, over time, coaching is becoming much more widely used to help develop the skills of "high potentials" – high performing, fully engaged employees who have been identified as potential future organizational leaders. What we're suggesting in this book, is that coaching is still underutilized as a powerful tool for increasing the engagement of the middle majority of employees out there – the 3 out of 5 employees who are only partially engaged in their work. Our goal is to encourage you and to equip you to join the many managers we've worked with in starting to use coaching conversations with as many of your employees as possible.

The Importance of Building Trust

No discussion of coaching as a manager is complete without touching on the crucial topic of trust. At its core, the coaching relationship between a manager and an employee is an exchange of trust. The manager is placing trust in the employee's creativity, resourcefulness, and competence. The employee is placing trust in the manager's commitment to the employee's development.

Under traditional directive styles of management, there is an inherent mistrust built into the manager-employee relationship. Employees are used to having their performance monitored, assessed, evaluated. Any admission of a lack of confidence, competence or judgement on the employee's part can be used against them. As a result, employees don't flag these opportunities for learning and growth.

It's no wonder, then, that when a manager begins to shift their style to incorporate coaching, they have to cope with initial resistance from staff who are suspicious of any departure from the existing style of management. In other words, it takes time to establish the foundation of trust that allows for successful coaching.

There are three things you can do to help accelerate trust building:

1. ***Demonstrate genuine care for your employee as a person.*** This involves getting to know a bit about their life and interests beyond work

(if you haven't already). Follow-up on what they shared with you in previous conversations and ask how things are going.

2. ***Be transparent about the fact that you are now wearing two hats***. You can clarify that you will still wear your manager hat which keeps you focused on business results and what's best for the organization. At the same time, you'll be adding a coach hat which will help you focus on their learning, growth, development and success. You'll also want to clarify how coaching fits into the performance management process. Wearing your manager hat, you'll still be setting performance expectations and ensuring their commitment to them. Wearing your coaching hat, you'll be helping them grow and develop to accomplish those expectations. This will involve taking advantage of learning opportunities as they occur, in real-time.

3. ***Involve them in your learning process***. Be open about the fact that coaching is an area of learning and growth for you. Let them know you are actively practicing your new coaching skills and ask them for feedback to help you improve. Act on that feedback to the best of your ability. By doing this, you are role modeling the process of learning on the job, with the support of colleagues (which is what you'll be offering them the chance to do as you coach them).

In Part III of the book, we'll return to this subject as an important part of getting started as a manager-coach. For now, we just want to plant the idea that it can take a bit of time to build a foundation of trust to support coaching. This is part of making the transition to a coaching style.

Next in Part II, we'll take a step-by-step walk through each of the core skills of the Coaching for Engagement™ model, giving you examples and practical tools you can start using right away.

What to Take Away from This Chapter

- Helping people think through problems rather than telling them what to do can feel unfamiliar and uncomfortable for managers initially. The payoff comes when you help an employee find the answer themselves, and they build their self-awareness, creativity, resourcefulness and competence.

- Any awkwardness managers experience when coaching initially is simply the awkwardness we all experience when we're practicing a new skill – not a sign they are somehow innately unsuited to coaching.

- Coaching does require an up-front investment of your time in order to gain time in the long-run (as employees become more self-reliant over time).

- The key to balancing your agenda as a manager (focusing on employees' performance) and as a coach (focusing on helping employees achieve choice, growth and purpose in their work) is to adopt a "both/and" mindset instead of getting caught in "either/or" thinking.

- There are some conditions that need to be in place for coaching to work as a management style: the employee is open to being coached, the employee is open to being coached by you, and the employee has an adequate level of knowledge, skill and ability on which to build.

- Situations characterized by "real urgency" are not the best time to initiate coaching.

- Trust is crucial to the success of the coaching relationship.

- Coaching involves an exchange of trust between a manager and an employee. The manager is placing trust in the employee's creativity, resourcefulness and competence. The employee is placing trust in the manager's commitment to the employee's development.

As a manager you can accelerate trust by demonstrating genuine care for your employees, being transparent about the fact that you are wearing two hats (manager and coach), and involving them in your learning process as you practice your coaching skills.

PART II: CORE COACHING SKILLS

"Mountains cannot be surmounted except by winding paths."

- Johann Wolfgang von Goethe

Chapter 3

Coaching Conversations Trailmap

In this part of the book, we walk you through the Coaching Conversation Trailmap – a path through six core coaching skills or competencies. The map is a variation on the Tekara Results Peak™ that we presented in Chapter 1, showing how individual self-awareness and energy management[1] leads to having better conversations, and how those conversations build positive relationships that in turn fuel the kind of engagement required to produce high performance and business results.

The Coaching Conversations Trailmap (Figure 3) starts at the bottom or base of the peak. Building on a strong foundation of self-awareness and energy management (coaching skill #1), it leads through a C.O.A.C.H. approach that includes five other skills (coaching skills #2, 3, 4, 5 and 6):

Curious Questioning

Open Listening

Appreciative Discovery

Catalytic Feedback

Heightened Engagement.

---

[1] In this book, we use the term "energy" in a very specific way. Energy is our capacity to perform work. Although we often think of our competence or skills as the key ingredients of our work performance, we also have to have the physical, emotional and mental energy (capacity) and motivation in the moment to execute the skill. Energy management, then, refers to the variety of ways that we can build and maintain the energy we need to perform well.

Figure 3: Coaching Conversations Trailmap

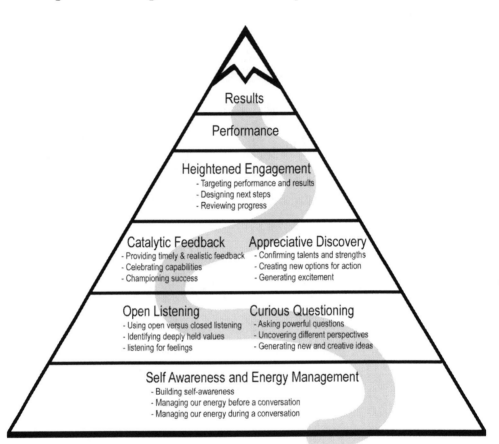

For each of the six coaching skills, we've identified three areas of focus (see Table 3 on next page).

Table 3: Overview of the Six Core Coaching Skills

Coaching Skill	Areas of Focus
Self-Awareness and Energy Management	**Building self-awareness** – noticing the energy we bring into a coaching conversation and how it fluctuates during the conversation **Managing our energy before a conversation** – preparing physically, emotionally and mentally, and clarifying your purpose and intention for the conversation **Managing our energy during a conversation** – striving to maintain a positive physical, emotional and mental state and reminding yourself about your intention for the conversation
Curious Questioning	**Asking powerful questions** – seeking to understand what others assume, value, and want to accomplish **Uncovering different perspectives** – being genuinely curious about what others think **Generating new and creative ideas** – sparking the kind of innovative thinking that produces new ways of seeing things and new possibilities
Open Listening	**Using open versus closed listening** – remaining respectful of what others are really saying and want to contribute (not just listening for what you want to hear or have them do) **Identifying deeply held values** – listening for the values and aspirations that motivate others most powerfully **Listening for feelings** – respecting the deeper agenda by listening for the things that matter most to others
Appreciative Discovery	**Confirming talents and strengths** – looking for the unique capacities and genius of others, so you can build together on their best **Creating new options for action** – exploring opportunities to channel talents and strengths in service of the organization's goals **Generating excitement about positive possibilities** – connecting with a strong source of motivation
Catalytic Feedback	**Providing timely and realistic feedback** – being real about what will help achieve success and what will get in the way **Championing successes** – setting small, high-leverage goals that have a good chance of being achieved **Celebrating capabilities** – catching someone doing something right and reinforcing it with praise to provide the incentive for further improvement
Heightened Engagement	**Targeting performance and results** – ensuring alignment with organizational goals **Designing next steps** – clarifying actions to be taken, anticipating potential obstacles, building commitment and agreeing on how progress will be reviewed **Reviewing progress** – identifying transferable learning and celebrating achievements

In Chapters 5 through 10, we'll cover one skill at a time in detail, providing you with practical tools you can start using immediately. But before diving into the skills, we're going to spend the next chapter looking at four key mindset shifts that we need to make in order to really get the skills working for us.

What to Take Away from This Chapter

- There are six core coaching skills we believe contribute to successful coaching conversations.

- Skillful coaching begins with building our self-awareness and managing our own energy before and during conversations so that we can fully present (Skill #1).

- Curious Questioning (Skill #2) involves asking powerful questions, uncovering different perspectives, and generating new and creative ideas.

- Open Listening (Skill #3) involves hearing what others are really saying, identifying deeply held values, and listening for feelings.

- Appreciative Discovery (Skill #4) involves confirming talents and strengths, explore new opportunities for applying those talents and strengths, and generating excitement about new possibilities.

- Catalytic Feedback (Skill #5) involves providing timely and realistic feedback, celebrating capabilities, setting achievable goals for improvement.

- The final skill (#6) involves translating Heightened Engagement into successful action by targeting performance and results, designing next steps, and reviewing progress.

"Coaching...is a different way of viewing people, a far more optimistic way than most of us are accustomed to, and it results in a different way of treating them. It requires us to suspend limiting beliefs about people, including ourselves, abandon old habits and liberate   ourselves from redundant ways of thinking."

- John Whitmore

Chapter 4

The Mindset of a Coach: Four Key Shifts

Change happens when we do something differently – or look at something differently. The chapters that follow (5 through 10) all focus on *doing* something differently – practicing a set of core coaching skills. This chapter is about *looking at* something differently – whether it's the employee, the problem we're trying to solve with them, or our role in the conversation.

The Four Key Mindset Shifts

We've noticed there are four key shifts in attitude and perspective that managers make in the process of adopting a coaching style (see Table 4). These shifts make the difference between a coaching conversation and a typical workplace conversation.

Table 4: Four Key Mindset Shifts of Effective Coaches

	From	To
Mindset Shift #1	Treating colleagues as lacking and inadequate	Treating colleagues as creative, resourceful and capable
Mindset Shift #2	Assuming that you already know	Listening for what your colleagues know
Mindset Shift #3	Telling people what to do	Asking people how they want to contribute
Mindset Shift #4	Trying to understand the underlying causes of a problem	Finding a solution to the problem

Let's take a closer look at each one.

Coaching for Engagement

Mindset Shift #1 – Treating Colleagues as Creative, Resourceful and Capable

If you think of your colleagues or direct reports as lacking or inadequate you'll see them as a problem or challenge to be managed. If you think of them as creative, resourceful and capable, you'll see them as a resource to be tapped – someone you could partner and collaborate with. And how you see them will affect how you treat them – and how you treat them will in large part determine how they perform.

It's called the Pygmalion Effect, also known as the self-fulfilling prophecy. We form expectations of people; we communicate those expectations with various cues (consciously or not, we tip people off); people tend to respond to these cues by adjusting their behaviour to match them; the result is that the original expectation becomes true. Here are just a few of the cues[9] – many of them subtle and unconscious on our part – that colleagues and direct reports pick up on that send the message that they're not a high performer in your eyes:

- Paying less attention to them (smiling less often and maintaining less eye contact)

- Giving them less information about what's going on in the department

- Calling on them less often to work on special projects, state their opinions, or give presentations

- Waiting less time for them to make their point or state their opinion during a discussion; interrupting them more often

- Providing less help or giving less advice to them when they really need it

- Criticizing them more frequently than high performers for making mistakes

- Praising them less frequently than high performers after successful efforts

46

- Praising them more frequently than high performers for marginal or inadequate effort

- Providing them with less accurate and less detailed feedback on job performance than high performers

- Demanding less work and effort from them than from high performers.

Conversely, what might you do differently – especially when you're coaching – if you were acting on the belief that the person you're speaking with is creative, resourceful and capable? Let's look at a short story, contrasting how two shift managers handle a conversation about a similar problem at work (Box 1 – next page).

The first shift manager's assumption that the operator is resourceful and capable is reflected in his question: 'What have you done so far?' In this case, the operator has only just noticed the problem – but you can be sure that next time, he'll be more likely to do some additional trouble-shooting before approaching the shift manager – because he'll be expecting the same question again. When the manager asks what the operator thinks he should do next, he continues to hold on to his belief that the operator is creative, resourceful and capable and will come up with some valid ideas about next steps and appropriate actions. Sure enough, the operator lives up to the manager's positive expectations.

Box 1: Comparing Two Different Management Approaches[10]

I once watched one of my shift managers coach an operator who came to report a fault on his machine. When the operator explained the problem, the shift manager asked 'What have you done so far?'

The operator said that he had just noticed the problem. The manager asked what he thought he should do next and the operator said, 'I will find the maintenance guy and see if we can fix it; if not, I will call out the control engineer from the other site.'

The manager asked, 'And what can you be doing in the meantime until the maintenance guy arrives?' The operator suggested he could help on another production line. The operator proposed all of the actions and the ownership was clear throughout.

A few days later, I watched a different shift manager dealing with a similar issue. When the operator reported the problem, the shift manager suggested 'Have you checked the optical sensors?'

The operator went away and soon returned to say, 'It's not the sensors.' At this, the shift manager went out to look for himself.

A few minutes after this, I saw the shift manager working on the machine – the operator had gone for a coffee! The shift manager had taken responsibility for the problem rather than helping the operator think it through for himself.

The difference? The first shift manager had discovered coaching.

By contrast, the second shift manager's questions and actions reflect an assumption that the operator is not capable of diagnosing the problem and not resourceful enough to resolve the problem himself. The result is the operator disengages from the problem altogether, no doubt cementing the second shift manager's perception of him as inadequate and lacking when it comes to problem solving. The operator lives up to the manager's negative expectations.

Mindset Shift #2 – Listening for What Your Colleagues Know

We make assumptions all the time – here's where it can get us into trouble and cause us to miss out. Have a look at the quadrant below (based on a tool called the Johari Window[11]):

What we both know	What you know that I don't know
What I know that you don't know	What neither of us knows

This mindset trap – assuming that we already know – creates one of several distortions in our thinking:

- the "what we both know" box is bigger than it really is (i.e., assuming that we are on the same wavelength or mean the same thing when we don't)

- the "what I know that you don't know" box is huge

- the "what you know that I don't know" box is very small (or nonexistent!)

- the "what neither of us knows" box doesn't exist – or doesn't matter.

When we're caught in any of these thought distortions, we stop asking about our colleagues' knowledge, insights and perspectives and rely heavily on "telling mode" – or just forging ahead without input or collaboration ("*I know best*," and "*I know how to handle this*").

Let's see how this mindset shift is at work in the shift manager and operator story. The first shift manager (using a coaching style) focused first on exploring the "what you know that I don't know box." He asked the operator what he knew about a possible solution: what had he already tried or thought of? Or, what could he think of? By contrast, the second shift manager immediately assumed he already knew what the most likely cause of the problem was. When his first guess was wrong, he saw no reason to continue the conversation with the operator – assuming the operator had no further knowledge or insight to offer – and went to figure it out for himself.

Here's how to reverse the trend when we catch ourselves falling into this trap:

1. Look for ways to expand the "what we both know" box by asking for others to share "what you know that I don't know." Test assumptions with others. Get curious. Ask questions like: What data and information do you have about the situation? What are the implications from your perspective? What is the significance of that? Where does your thinking/reasoning go next? What opportunities or solutions does it suggest to you? What else have you thought of? In addition to having face to face conversations to grow the "what we both know" box, you can also solicit feedback in other ways; for example, using a 360 degree feedback process to collect information about performance, or creating an anonymous online employee suggestion box.

2. Shrink the "what neither of us knows" box by asking questions like: What other factors should be considered? Who else might have useful knowledge, insight, perspective about this?

One manager with whom we've worked (and who asked to remain anonymous about this admission!) talks somewhat sheepishly about his mindset shift in this area and the impact of asking his team for more input and ideas: *"It made me better because when I got their advice – gee! – sometimes it really worked. As outrageous to me as it might have seemed, somebody knew better than me in a particular situation!"*

Mindset Shift #3 – Asking People How They Want To Contribute

If you have to figure out what your colleagues or direct reports should be doing all the time, that's exhausting. As soon as they follow through on your latest set of instructions, they'll be back for more direction. Whenever you're not telling them what to do, they assume it's okay for them to disengage.

When your mindset is based on the assumption that your role as manager is to tell others what to do, they will wait on the sidelines until you do.

If instead, you ask them where and how they want to contribute – use their talents and strengths to pull along side you in the direction the organization is heading – then something different happens. They share the responsibility for figuring out how to contribute, instead of you having to shoulder it all. They're also far more likely to come up with a way of contributing that is motivating for them. They know best what engages them in their work.

Let's return to our story about the shift managers and operators. Using a coaching style, the first shift manager asked the operator what he could be doing to stay productive (contribute) while he was waiting for the maintenance guy to arrive. The operator suggested he help on another production line. Had the manager decided for the operator what he should do in the meantime, chances are the operator would have done it, but grudgingly – we all prefer to be given choice, whenever possible. The second shift manager got into the telling cycle. When the operator came to him with the problem, he told him to go check and see if the problem was X. When it wasn't X – and when the shift manager got busy trying to figure it out for himself – the operator just retreated to the sidelines, waiting to be told what to do next.

Think of a time when a manager gave you the latitude to shape your contribution to a project or initiative (instead of telling you what to do). Think about how much more motivated and engaged you were as a result. That's what this mindset shift is about.

Mindset Shift #4 – Focusing on Finding a Solution

Instead of spending valuable time searching for the cause of the problem (which may or may not suggest a solution), this shift invites us to focus instead on the future we want to create, and how we can learn from what's already going well to create a path to get there. Since no problem occurs all the time, the direct route to a solution lies in identifying what is going on when the problem is not present, and then amplifying that.

When we focus on finding a solution, we ask questions like:

- "What's working well already?"

- "When are we successful at it? When is the problem not present? Under what conditions?"

- "What's different about those times?"

- "How can we make those times happen more often?"

This generates a very different kind of conversation than if we are focused on understanding the problem, in which case we might ask question like:

- "What's not working?"

- "Why isn't it working?"

- "Where did we go wrong?"

- "Who's to blame for it not working?"

The first set of questions is also much more likely to generate energy, enthusiasm and cooperation. It's also consistent with an approach that seeks to create positive results, rather than just focus on the negative or the problem.

Consider the following example:

> *A member of staff reports that they find a particular customer difficult. They know it is illogical, because they are older and more experienced than the customer, but when they think of meeting with them they feel nervous and, predictably, meetings do not go well. A problem focused approach would be to probe, 'Why?' The conversation could then move into a fascinating exploration of the customer's similarities with a key person in the staff member's past. The staff member could leave the meeting feeling happier for having recognized the similarity, but no more equipped to handle the next meeting any differently. The discussion may simply have magnified the*

issue by reinforcing the links in their mind between two problematic people.

A solution focused approach would help them [the staff member] find ways of incorporating different behaviours into their encounters with the customer. It could do this by getting them to think of other difficult customers where they have managed to improve the relationship, and identifying what they did to bring about the change. Or, the staff member would be encouraged to think of the best encounter they ever had with the customer and what they did that made that encounter less painful, so that they can replicate the conditions.

The success of the next meeting [with the customer] will then be based on having drawn their attention to resources they can readily access, without them ever needing to understand why the relationship is problematic. In making the meeting more successful than previous meetings, the dynamics of the relationship will have begun to change. [12]

The bottom line is that you can solve a problem without understanding its cause in detail.

Making the Shifts: Acting "As If"

So how do you start to make these shifts in mindset? It turns out a fast and effective way is to start acting "as if" you had that mindset.[13] Pick any one of the mindsets and then ask yourself: *"If I had that mindset, how would I act? How would I treat the other person in the conversation? What kinds of questions would I ask?"* To help you with this, Table 5 provides some initial ideas.

Table 5: Suggestions for Putting the Mindset Shifts in to Action

Mindset	Things You Might Do	Questions You Might Ask
1. Treating colleagues as creative, resourceful and capable	Catching people doing something right Praising them more frequently after successful efforts	What have you done so far (to solve the problem)? What do you think you could do next? What options can you think of? I've seen you do this well before; how did you do it then? How could you build on that?
2. Listening for what your colleagues know	Interrupt less often; listen more openly Sharing information more freely and asking others to do the same	What data and information do you have about the situation? What are the implications from your perspective? What is the significance of that? Where does your thinking/reasoning go next? What opportunities or solutions does it suggest to you? What else have you thought of? What other factors should be considered? Who else might have useful knowledge, insight and perspective about this?
3. Asking people how they want to contribute	Noticing what people excel at (where their particular strengths/talents lie) Calling on them more often to work on special projects, state their opinions, or give presentation	What role would you like to play in this? What can the team count on you to contribute to the project? How do you see yourself using your previous experience with _____ to help us with this?
4. Finding a solution to the problem	Avoid asking questions that start with "Why?" Maintain a solutions focus: ask questions that identify what is most likely to be successful/helpful	What's working well already? When are we successful at it? When is the problem not present? Under what conditions? What's different about those times? How can we make those times happen more often?

Checking Your Mindset at the Door

One helpful habit to build as you practice coaching is to do a quick assessment of your mindset as you head into a coaching conversation:

- What mindsets are you walking in with (in the "From" column)?

- Which one mindset shift do you most need to focus on during this conversation?

- How could you equip yourself to stick with that shift through the conversation? What questions could you prepare and jot down ahead of time to help you stay in that more positive mindset?

	From	To
Mindset Shift #1	Treating colleagues as lacking and inadequate	Treating colleagues as creative, resourceful and capable
Mindset Shift #2	Assuming that you already know	Listening for what your colleagues know
Mindset Shift #3	Telling people what to do	Asking people how they want to contribute
Mindset Shift #4	Trying to understand the underlying causes of a problem	Finding a solution to the problem

For example, if your focus is Mindset #1 or #3, how will you phrase your questions in ways which invite them to provide input and demonstrate how their ideas can contribute?

If your focus is Mindset #2, where might you be making assumptions about other people's thinking? What curious questions could you ask to test those assumptions and learn more about their relevant knowledge and perspective?

What to Take Away from This Chapter

- There are four key shifts in perspective and attitude that managers make in the process of adopting a coaching style.

- The first shift is from treating colleagues as lacking and inadequate, to treating them as creative, resourceful and capable.

- The second shift is from assuming that you already know everything you need to know, to assuming that your colleagues know something different, helpful and useful (and that your job is to elicit their knowledge and ideas).

- The third shift is from telling people what to do, to asking people how they want to contribute.

- The fourth and final shift is from trying to understand the history and underlying causes of a problem, to finding a solution to the problem.

"Manage yourself,
so others won't have to."

- John Wooden

Chapter 5

Skill # 1: Self-Awareness and Energy Management

You might be tempted to skip over this first skill and just move straight into the other five skills that make up the C.O.A.C.H. approach – but we urge you to pay attention to this one. With a strong foundation of self-awareness and energy management, you'll be far more effective at applying all of the other skills.

In this chapter, we'll cover three related areas of focus:

- **Building self-awareness** by noticing the energy we bring into a coaching conversation and how it fluctuates during the conversation

- **Managing our energy before a conversation** by preparing physically, emotionally and mentally, and clarifying your purpose and intention for the conversation

- **Managing our energy during a conversation** by striving to maintain a positive physical, emotional and mental state and reminding yourself about your intention for the conversation.

Coaching starts with your presence – being fully immersed in the conversation you're having. Not being worried about the past. Not being worried about the future. Just present with what is happening right here, right now. Easy to say, hard to do. Leaders who are able to do this well are extremely engaging, partly because true presence is so rare.

What does it take to cultivate the kind of presence needed to coach well? Two intertwined skills: self-awareness and energy management.

Self-awareness simply describes our ability to be aware of the energy we bring into a coaching conversation and to notice how it fluctuates during the conversation. Your ability to bring all your attention and awareness to observing yourself is also sometimes referred to as mindfulness. Observing your mindset (discussed in the previous chapter) heading into a conversation or meeting is an example of self-awareness; noticing yourself tense up (around your jaw or in your shoulders) in response to a provocative comment during a conversation is another.

Energy management is the ability to do something about whatever you notice through self-awareness. More specifically, to cultivate more positive, productive energy in your coaching conversations, and to let go of any unhelpful energy so that it doesn't limit you, the employee, or the conversation. Consciously choosing to shift your mindset is one example of energy management; pausing and taking a deep breath before responding to a challenging comment is another.

What Do We Mean by Energy? How Can We Become More Aware of Our Energy?

In this book, we use the term "energy" in a very specific way.[14] Energy is our capacity to perform work. Although we often think of our competence or skills as the key ingredients of our work performance, we also have to have the capacity (energy) in the moment to execute the skill.

But let's back up. Imagine that you are an energy system – a complex and sophisticated one – running on four distinct, yet inter-connected types of energy: physical, emotional, mental, and 'spiritual'. Table 6 provides a quick overview of all four, along with an idea of what to begin noticing – or become self-aware of – about each one.

Table 6: Four Types of Energy & Tips for Building Self-Awareness

Type of Energy and Description	How to Build Self-Awareness of This Type of Energy
Physical energy is the overall quantity of energy you bring to the conversation. Your physical energy 'fuel tank' will be more or less full depending on how we move and breathe, what and how often we eat, and the amount of rest and recovery you give yourself throughout the day.	How tired or energized are you overall? How are you breathing? Are your muscles tense or relaxed? What is your heart rate? Do you have the sensation of hot or cold anywhere in your body? What posture are you in? How does your voice sound? Is there anything going on for you physically that is distracting you?
Emotional energy is the quality of your energy you bring to the conversation, shaped by the emotions you feel – and cultivate. Some emotional states will help you to be effective in your coaching; others will take you off track and may even 'leak' out and infect the other person.	How connected do you feel to your own emotions? What do you feel: Anxious? Excited? Disgusted? Optimistic? Hurt? Engaged? Angry? Disappointed? Hopeful? Frustrated? Inspired?
Mental energy is the focus of your energy during the conversation. Your level of mental energy will influence your ability to concentrate, to shift your attention flexibly between noticing what's going on for you and what's going on for your employee, to truly listen and hear what your employee is saying, and to formulate powerful questions to ask your employee.	What's got your attention in this moment? How focused or distracted are you? How easily are you able to concentrate on what your employee is saying?
'Spiritual' energy is not esoteric or religious – but rather the force and direction of your energy. You can also think of it as the sense of purpose, shaped by your character and values. It can vary in intensity depending on how clear you are about what matters most to you (at work and in life more generally) – and how well your choices and behaviours align with that.	How clear are you about your purpose in having this coaching conversation? What values are important to you and the person you're coaching?

Our levels of energy in each of the four areas are always fluctuating, depending on what is happening around us and the choices we make about how to manage our energy in response. Picture a dashboard, with one meter for each kind of energy. If you were in a great state for a coaching conversation, the dials would read: physically energized, emotionally connected, mentally focused, and 'spiritually' aligned with what matters most.

Why is This Important in the Context of Having Coaching Conversations?

The quantity, quality, focus and force of the energy we bring can either create a safe and powerful space for conversation, or quickly derail it. Managing our own energy is the foundation for every successful coaching conversation.

Let's look first at the combined impact of our physical and emotional energy on our coaching (Figure 4). When our physical energy is high and the quality of our emotions is positive (quadrant B in the diagram), we are usually in an ideal state to coach. Managers often describe feeling fully engaged, excited, creative, and inspired in this state. But it is impossible to stay in this quadrant all the time. As our physical energy drops (we get tired, hungry, stiff, etc.), we need a break to recover and renew (quadrant D). If we listen and respond to that need, we can get back into the high performance quadrant again very quickly. If we don't, we drift over to the left hand quadrants (A and C) where survival-based emotions begin to kick in.

Here's an example. A client of ours, an executive in an investment firm, travels frequently to over half a dozen offices around North America. His colleagues described him as critical, and perfectionist. His frustration and impatience easily boiled up into anger. He then became quite vocal about his anger. Obviously it was pretty challenging for him to have productive conversations when he was in that state. Before tackling the other core coaching skills (discussed in the chapters that follow), this executive needed to start by working on his self-awareness and energy management. First, he needed to become more aware of when he was becoming angry (slipping into survival mode). Then, he needed to practice managing his energy - shifting himself back into an emotional state that would be a better starting place for conversations.

Figure 4: Link Between Physical and Emotional Energy[15]

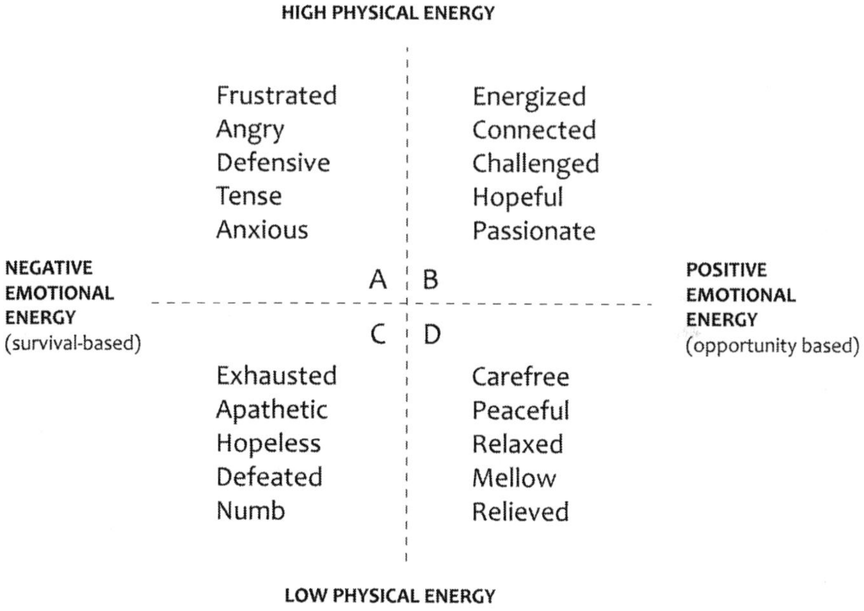

HIGH PHYSICAL ENERGY

	Frustrated		Energized
	Angry		Connected
	Defensive		Challenged
	Tense		Hopeful
	Anxious		Passionate

NEGATIVE EMOTIONAL ENERGY (survival-based) — — — — — — — — — — — — A ¦ B — — — — — — — — — POSITIVE EMOTIONAL ENERGY (opportunity based)

C ¦ D

	Exhausted		Carefree
	Apathetic		Peaceful
	Hopeless		Relaxed
	Defeated		Mellow
	Numb		Relieved

LOW PHYSICAL ENERGY

Clearly, as coaches, we want to do whatever we can to prevent ourselves from drifting into the survival quadrants. But no matter how masterful we are, we will find ourselves there from time to time. The key is how quickly we recognize the shift or drift when it is occurring – and how quickly we respond to start creating a shift back to a more positive state.

Helpful Habits for Preparing for a Coaching Conversation

We talked earlier about the ideal state to be in when you head into a coaching conversation: physically energized, emotionally connected (to yourself and the other person), mentally focused, and spiritually aligned with what matters most. What can you do ahead of time to get yourself there – physically, emotionally, mentally and spiritually? Table 7 summarizes some energy management tips you can use to prepare yourself for a successful coaching conversation.

Table 7: Practical Tips for Managing Your Energy Before Heading Into a Coaching Conversation

Physical	***Make sure you've eaten in the last 2 to 3 hours – if not, grab a bite.*** If you haven't had anything to eat in the last 2 to 3 hours, your body is already going into survival mode, and is beginning to shut down certain mental functions. Emotionally it's triggering chemical reactions that are going to make it much more difficult to be engaged in the conversation. ***Get up and move.*** Have you gotten up and moved in the last 90 minutes – or have you been sitting in your chair for an extended period of time? When it comes to fueling our brains to function well during a coaching conversation, we need both glucose (sugar) and oxygen. Food gives us the glucose; movement gets oxygen circulating. If you want to be at your best, take a walk around the building, climb a flight of stairs, raise your heart rate for a few minutes, or go outside and take some deep breaths. ***Be mindful of the time of day when scheduling the conversation.*** For many of us, we hit a lull in our physical energy around 2 to 3 pm – it's part of the circadian rhythm or wake/sleep cycle we experience every 24 hours. Whenever your daily low point is, avoid that time slot for coaching conversations if at all possible. If you do need to have it then, you may need to spend a few minutes beforehand to boost your energy by moving or doing some active breathing. You might even consider having your coaching conversation while walking together, if your employee is open to it.
Emotional	***Clear the emotional decks.*** Take a moment to do a quick scan of your emotional energy. If you're feeling relaxed, optimistic, and hopeful, then you're in an ideal state to coach. If on the other hand you're feeling tense, anxious, frustrated, worried, or overwhelmed, the challenge is not to carry that into your conversation. How do you shift your emotional state? Here are a couple of suggestions for things you could do in as few as 2-3 minutes that can have a big impact: • close your eyes and think of something that brings you joy (e.g., fun times, the face of a loved one, a hilarious situation that made you laugh, a place you enjoyed visiting, etc.) *cont...*

Emotional (cont.)	• briefly listen to some music you enjoy • close your eyes and picture a point in the not-to-distant future when you'll have some relief from the emotions that are weighing on you (e.g., how much fun you'll have when the weekend comes; how good you'll feel when you finally have that talk with your boss; how good you'll feel when the speech you're so worried about is finally over; how good you'll feel when the day is done and you're finally snuggled down in bed ready to sleep) We often underestimate how effective these small acts can be in shifting our emotional energy.
Mental	*Minimize interruptions.* Make sure that you will not be interrupted during your coaching session. Turn off your computer screen and the volume on your computer speakers, turn off your cell phone (unless you are specifically "on-call"), *Park the distractions.* In your mind's eye, picture taking anything that is vying for your attention and putting it in a drawer. Close this imaginary drawer knowing that you can take everything out again after your coaching session. *Picture yourself coaching successfully.* See yourself coaching as if you were watching a movie of yourself from the audience (rather than imagining yourself looking out from the eyes of the actor). In as much detail as possible, picture how you will move, how you will stand/sit and hold your shoulders and upper body, how and where your eyes will be focused, what you will sound like, what your facial expression will be like. The more detail you add and notice, the more likely you will embody all that during your actual coaching session.
Spiritual	*Get clear on what you hope to accomplish in the conversation.* Take a moment to reflect. What would make this coaching conversation a success? What are you hoping to learn? What are you hoping to practice? What impact are you hoping it will have on your relationship with the person you're coaching?

Learning to Bounce Back in the Moment: Recovering During a Coaching Conversation

So, you've done what you can to prepare for a successful coaching conversation ahead of time. Now, what do you need to do to stay physically energized, emotionally connected, mentally focused and aligned with what matters most during a session? It comes down to finding small ways of staying on track.

Professional athletes train themselves to be great at this. In tennis, for example, up to 80% of a player's success depends on what they do between points, when they have 20 to 30 seconds to recover and prepare for the next flurry of activity. Well trained tennis players use this time strategically by actively focusing on how to renew their capacity in all four areas – physical, emotional, mental, and spiritual. For example:

1. To renew their **physical** energy, they use active breathing techniques to lower their heart rate back to the ideal zone and to increase oxygen flow to their brain and muscles. Muscle tension release techniques, stretching, and walking all promote recovery and readiness for the next point.

2. Regardless of what happened in the point that just finished, they make an effort to get back to a positive (or at least neutral) **emotional** state. They focus on having fun out there, and not letting a high or low moment take too much of their energy. Much of this connects with the mental dimension, and what the athlete chooses to think about in the moment.

3. In 20 to 30 seconds a lot can happen cognitively. Where will they choose to focus their **mental** energy: the past, the future, or the present moment? Rather than focusing on what just happened (in the past) or what they hope will happen (in the future), high performance athletes focus on what needs to happen in this present moment.

4. To regain their **'spiritual'** footing, they remind themselves why they are on the court: *"What am I really trying to accomplish here? What's my purpose?"* For most athletes it has to be about more than winning – it's about the core values that both drive them to perform and shape who they are. As soon as an athlete can no longer connect to this, all three of the other dimensions will begin to unravel, often resulting in the loss of the match.

What's the equivalent for you as a manager-coach? Table 8 captures some ideas on how to keep yourself in an ideal state for coaching throughout the conversation.

Table 8: Practical Tips for Managing Your Energy During a Coaching Conversation

Physical	*Breathe.* When stressed, we tend to take short, shallow breaths. This reduces our capacity for engaging fully in the moment. It reduces the amount of oxygen our brain has access too, and makes it easier to slip into survival mode. Remind yourself to just breathe! When you sense any tension in your neck or jaw, or someone has said something provocative and you get a rush of emotion, take a deep breath before responding. This 5 second pause can be enough to regain your composure, or reset yourself to ensure you are focused on the opportunity in the conversation again.
Emotional	*Stay positive.* If you feel yourself getting tense, anxious, frustrated, or angry, draw on your physical energy by breathing (as suggested above) to create a positive shift. If you really need to, take a break. Tell the other person you need to take a time-out so that you can be more helpful to them, and agree on a time to reconvene.
Mental	*Direct your focus.* Choose to focus on the present, instead of on the past (whatever just happened) or the future (what you hope will or will not happen). What needs to happen in <u>this</u> moment?
Spiritual	*Remember why you're having this conversation.* What's my purpose here? What values do I want to demonstrate in the way I interact during this conversation?

All of these suggestions for managing your energy either before or during a coaching conversation can also be thought of as "performance rituals." In Part IV of the book, we will explore this topic further when we dive into developing your development plan as a coach.

What to Take Away from This Chapter

- Excellent coaching begins with presence, which is fuelled by self-awareness and personal energy management.

- As coaches (and as humans), we have four distinct but interconnected kinds of energy circulating in us all the time – physical, emotional, mental, and 'spiritual'.

- The ideal coaching state involves being physically energized, emotionally connected, mentally focused, and 'spiritually' aligned with what matters most.

- There are a variety of simple but effective practices you can adopt to successfully manage your energy both before and during a coaching conversation.

"The important thing is not to stop questioning ... Never lose a holy curiosity."

- Albert Einstein

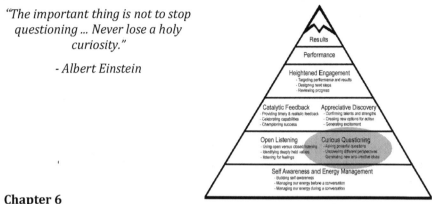

Chapter 6

Skill #2: Curious Questioning

Think back to the last conversation you had with someone when you could tell they were genuinely curious about you and your world. Their curiosity probably encouraged you to let your guard down a bit, and reveal or share things about yourself more freely, further building your relationship with that person. Compare that memory with one where you felt you were being interrogated, diagnosed, or judged. That's the difference curiosity makes.

In this chapter, we'll cover three related aspects of Curious Questioning:

- *Asking powerful questions* as we seek to understand what others assume, value, and want to accomplish

- *Uncovering different perspectives* by being genuinely curious about what others think

- *Generating new and creative ideas* by sparking the kind of innovative thinking that produces new ways of seeing things and new possibilities.

But first, let's dispel a powerful myth that gets in the way of Curious Questioning.

Myth: As a Manager, You Need to Have All the Answers

You don't need to have all the answers. In fact, you there is no way that you could. Yet if you're like most of us, you probably still feel like you should. Why is that?

As managers, most of us receive years and years of training in being forceful, articulate advocates. Along the way we are praised for our ability to solve problems, answer every question, and give timely advice to others. That's why coaching – and particularly the initial step of asking more questions – can feel uncomfortable at first.

As a coach, our role is not to be the expert, the trouble shooter, or the consultant. We are not the rescuer, the guru, or the sage on the stage. When we decide to put on our "coaching hat," we become a *guide coming alongside* – exploring what a situation looks like from the perspective of the employee, and helping them to determine their best path forward. Doing that requires a deep commitment to staying curious.

But it's not just you thinking you need to have all the answers – your employees are trained to believe it too. It's only recently that we're starting to see a shift in the role of leaders – from being charismatic decision-makers and infallible bosses to becoming people who facilitate questioning and problem solving. So while trying on the "coaching hat" may feel uncomfortable for you at first, it will also feel different for your employees when they see you taking a different approach – helping them think through problems rather than doing the thinking for them.

So why coach if people just want an answer from you? Well, they do and they don't. People want to get unstuck, or generate the results that are eluding them. But they don't necessarily need to have the answer come from you – even if they ask for it! The best part about coaching is when it's successful, it generates results (an "answer") *and* deeper learning. Giving advice may generate short term results, but it can rob the people we lead of deeper learning and development. By getting caught in the trap of constantly giving advice, or trying to solve the problem, we can perpetuate a cycle that doesn't develop capacity of your team – not to mention consume more of your time and energy than is necessary.

As one of our clients (a CEO in the software industry) shared with us: "When I apply 'what?' and 'how?' [types of questions], and simply get curious, it results in more exploratory discussion and it results in the person taking ownership for the issue … it frees me from taking on the person's problem."[16]

By finding the answers for themselves, employees develop their self-awareness, capacity, intuition and resourcefulness. Deeper learning takes place when ownership of a solution comes from the employee, not us.

Sidebar 1: Ask Questions or Offer Advice?

Q. What if the person really wants advice? Isn't there ever a good time to give it?

It's a good question. Yes, there certainly is a time to offer advice in coaching but the temptation – and danger – is jumping to it too quickly. Through the interviews we've conducted with leaders and coaches for this book, we discovered many who use a combination approach: coaching first and then giving advice later. But the leaders and coaches who use that approach noted that the quality of their advice became much more valuable after unpacking the situation through Curious Questioning first.

For example, one leader described how he was looking for advice about the selection of board members and their roles in the newly developing structure. While the initial request was for advice about both aspects, after some clarifying and Curious Questioning, the advice that came from other well-seasoned leaders was better able to target the leader's underlying concerns. The combination – of questioning first and then giving advice after – worked well in this situation.

But rather than use this as an excuse to jump into advising when coaching is feeling a bit uncomfortable, we encourage leaders to really stretch. Let yourself experiment with the power of curious questions; see how far it takes you.

The Value of Curiosity

Curiosity is especially important in the early stages of a coaching conversation. An interesting pattern we've noticed is the first "issue" that an employee starts to talk about and discuss is not always the real issue. If you drill down a little – with some Curious Questioning – you will likely uncover another layer to the situation. Your curiosity may give the employee a fresh perspective or wider angle lens on their dilemma, as well as help them uncover solutions to the real underlying problem. As a result, they will be much further ahead than if you had jumped in to try and solve the first issue.

This is just one example of the way curiosity can help us challenge our assumptions – in the case above, we might have been stuck in the assumption that the first issue the employee presented was the real issue. Curious Questioning can help prevent us from getting caught by what we don't know.

Curiosity also enhances the relationship and builds trust – both your trust in them, and the employee's trust in themselves. The keys to this process are to be genuinely curious, and to not make those we coach feel as though he or she is being judged, interrogated, or manipulated. Try Exercise 1 as a way to get started.

Exercise 1: Practicing Curious Questioning

Have a 5-minute conversation with someone where all you do is ask them curious questions about whatever they want to talk about.

The ground rule is that you can't speak about yourself, or give them advice.

You can only ask questions (but avoid questions that start with "Why...?" since those can sometimes lead people to feel interrogated).

See what happens.....

In Box 2, we provide a few sample questions and phrases that can help you leverage another curious question to learn more. It's often not until we demonstrate this level of interest, by asking follow-up questions and seeking more detail, that people truly trust our desire to hear what they have to say.

Box 2: Sample Curious Questions and Queries

> You will be surprised how much more information you might get by following up any other curious question with one of these:
>
> - What's going on there?
> - What else?
> - Tell me more. Say more about that. Expand on that.
>
> You can also try combining an observation with a question or query. Repeat back the most significant thing the person said, using their exact words, and then encourage them to take it further:
>
> You mentioned that _____. Tell me more about it.

Next, a word about the mindset we need to adopt to be successful at Curious Questioning.

Mindset First

Asking curious questions begins by entering the conversation with a curious mindset rather than a diagnosing one. Nothing focuses someone's attention like a good question. But asking questions without a curious mindset can backfire if:

- You think you already know the answer to the question

- The question treats the individual like they are a child

- The question is a guise for leading someone to the solution you think is best

- The tone and pace of how a question is asked comes across as an interrogation

- You're not really listening to what the employee is communicating.

We all fall into these traps. Most leaders, especially those with a lot of experience in their line of work or a lot of knowledge from their schooling, pride themselves on their ability to gather information by asking specific questions to diagnose the problem, and to then come up with appropriate recommendations. But there is a big difference between diagnostic questions that elicit information and curious questions that evoke personal exploration.

How can you tell the difference? A tell-tale sign of a diagnosing mindset is that we ask a lot of closed-ended questions. If you want to cultivate a more curious mindset, focus on asking questions that invite a richer answer than just "Yes" or "No." Also, focus on allowing the employee to clarify their own thinking, rather than using questions to clarify your own understanding. You don't need to know the whole "story" before you help them advance their thinking.

Asking Powerful Questions

Powerful questions draw out other people's unique values, passions, assumptions, and perspectives. They provide an opportunity for your employee to let you know what they really feel, think, and desire. And interestingly, people don't always consciously know what they think and feel ahead of time so the answer to a powerful question is often a discovery for both individuals.

Powerful coaching questions share several common characteristics:

Table 9: Characteristics and Impact of Questions

Powerful Questions are:	Less Powerful Questions are:
Short	Long
Simple	Complex
Open ended (starting with how, what, who, when)	Multiple, serial
No "right" answer	Closed ended (yes/no response)
	Disguised solutions, recommendations, or advice
The result of powerful questions:	**The result of less powerful questions:**
Employee does the work	Coach does the work
Employee understands a bigger picture	Employee only gets coach's knowledge
Employee creates options	Employee gets resistant or defensive
Employee commits to action	Employee doesn't own actions

One of the ways we like to illustrate the difference between the impact of powerful open-ended questions and less powerful closed questions is to use the analogy of a backpack. During our Coaching for Engagement™ training program, we invite participants to guess what kind of object the instructor has put in a backpack sitting on a table at the front of the room. They are only allowed to ask closed questions – ones that can be answered with a "yes" or "no" response. This sets up a situation where a remarkably similar pattern is repeated with each group we work with. Some of the participants disengage fairly quickly, losing interest when they have a hard time identifying the object, frustrated by the limited information they get from the instructor's yes/no responses. Those who stay engaged start to ask remarkably similar questions, as if convinced they know what is in the backpack even when the instructor's responses clearly indicate they need to shift or broaden their thinking. And the instructor – as much as he would like to help the participants – is restricted by the format of the questions.

Now imagine you are a manager-coach and you are one of the participants, only in this case, you are trying to guess what is in your employee's "backpack." See how frustrating – and time-consuming – it will be for you and your employee if you are repeating that pattern. Now imagine how much more easily and quickly you can get the contents of the "backpack" out on the table if you are asking open-ended questions so that they can describe their concern, problem, opportunity, or aspiration. Box 3 provides you with examples of powerful questions.

Box 3: Sample Powerful Questions

> What is the challenge you're working on?
> How could you change the situation?
> What will that get you?
> How can you get the resources that you need?
> What are some options?
> What might get in your way?
> How would you deal with that?
> How will you know when you've been successful?

Sometimes, we feel uncomfortable asking powerful questions, especially if we're worried it might make us look dumb. Just remember that what can seem like the dumbest or simplest questions can unlock a conversation.

When we ask powerful, curious questions we begin to build awareness and self -responsibility in individuals we lead or work with. Notice that a lot of these questions start with "What" or "How." It takes some practice to move away from starting with "Why" to starting with "What" or "How" instead. The big benefit is that "What" and "How" seem to evoke less defensiveness in the employee, and keep a positive focus on the future.

Consider the following story demonstrating how a sequence of simple, powerful questions can challenge an employee's assumptions, encourage them to identify a solution, and motivate them to act:

Kay was ... [a junior manager] with responsibility for one section of the store. She had noticed that some produce was not selling and suspected it was the way it was displayed. She said nothing, however, because she assumed it was not her role, and that others would know better. One day, a regional manager visited the store and started to chat to her about her area. Feeling he had some interest, she asked him 'Do you think this layout works?' Expecting him to share his far greater knowledge of retailing by telling her what to do, she was surprised when he replied, 'What do you think isn't working?' She told him her perspective, in order that he would solve the problem, and was flattered when he responded, 'It sounds as though you understand what the problem is. What do you think we should change?' Emboldened, she told him. To which he replied, 'So, what is stopping you from doing it?' 'I did not think I could,' she responded. 'Who has told you not to use your initiative?' he questioned. To which the truthful response was 'No-one'... [This conversation] had a profound effect on her, not only at the time, but in her subsequent management of staff. What she had learnt ... was that a short interaction can have a big impact.[17]

We think you'll be pleasantly surprised about the positive effect of asking simple, well-chosen questions. What changes could you create if you began asking more powerful questions this week? In which conversations (with whom) would you start?

Uncovering Different Perspectives

Wouldn't it make work easier if everyone agreed with our perspective on everything all the time? The reality is, people interpret things differently based on their own values, beliefs, and experiences. Two people can even share the exact same experience together, and have completely different perspectives on it. Most of the time, we see this as a curse. But it's also a blessing. It's the reason that two heads are better than one whenever there's a problem to be solved.

So how do we get better at uncovering others' perspectives? To truly hear, we are best served by adopting what Albert Einstein called "a holy curiosity":

> *The important thing is not to stop questioning. Curiosity has its own reason for existing. One cannot help but be in awe when he contemplates the mysteries of eternity, of life, of the marvellous structure of reality. It is enough if one tries merely to comprehend a little of this mystery every day. Never lose a holy curiosity.[18]*

In the case of coaching for engagement, that curiosity is focused on the views, values, assumptions, and perspectives of the other people with whom you are working. If you can comprehend a little bit more of that mystery every day, you will have a much greater positive influence among your colleagues. Box 4 provides you with some sample questions you can use to learn more about someone else's perspective.

Box 4: Sample Questions for Discovering Other Perspectives

What's your thinking on that? Can you help me understand your perspective?

What causes you to say that?

What leads you to conclude that?

What data or experiences do you have that leads you to say/believe that?

What is the significance of that?

How does this relate to your other concerns?

Where does your reasoning go next?

How would your proposal affect _____?

How would this be similar to (or different from) _____?

Can you describe an example of that?

Perspectives can also be like "ruts" in our thinking. Leaders with a lot of experience, or people who are very opinionated (any of us, really), can get very stuck in those ruts. It's important that we challenge both ourselves and others to explore different perspectives before making judgements and decisions. A great question to ask in these situations is: "*What is another way to look at that issue?*" Box 5 provides some variations on this question.

Box 5: Sample Questions for Examining a Situation from Different Perspectives

If you were standing in the customers' shoes, what would look different?

If you were looking at this situation standing in the CEO's shoes, what would you see?

If you were looking back 3 to 6 months from now, what would your perspective on this situation be? How about 3 to 5 years from now?

If you were a fly on the wall, what would you notice about the situation?

Helping an employee shift their perspective allows them to get enough distance from their familiar way of thinking that they can come up with other possibilities. It's not important they commit to those new ideas; only that they understand there are other options that could be investigated.

Generating New and Creative Ideas

As a leader, we can spark innovation – by tapping people's creativity and resourcefulness – with the questions that we ask in our daily work. Curious Questioning keeps the lines of communication constantly open and helps a company or organization reach its full innovative potential. Box 6 presents some questions specifically designed to help someone free up their thinking and come up with different options.

Box 6: Sample Questions for Generating New and Creative Ideas Using SCAMPER Model[19]

How could you **substitute** some of the components, people, materials, or other resources that you are using right now for different ones?

How could you **combine** or blend products/services in a different way? What would a hybrid look like?

How could you **alter**, adapt, change the function, or use part of another element?

How could you **modify** (miniaturize, magnify) some aspect of your approach (e.g., increase or reduce the scale, change the shape, etc.)?

How could you put something to another use?

How could you **eliminate**, remove, or simplify one key element? How could you reduce something to its core functionality? What would happen if you got rid of some of the "extras?"

How could you **reverse** the order, switch roles, or rearrange (patterns, pace, etc.)?

During Curious Questioning, we're also creating a safe space for new and creative ideas to emerge and take root. Think of new plants when they are first emerging from the soil – at that stage, they're still very vulnerable and it doesn't take much to damage them or dislodge them. That's why it's so important to stick to one very important ground rule when brainstorming during a coaching session: no criticism, judgement, analysis or evaluation of ideas while they're being generated (that can happen later). Otherwise, their creativity will be stifled.

Here's how one football coach underscores the importance of creating an environment where ideas are welcomed and valued:

> *Ideas should be innocent until proven guilty...[but] some people think ideas are guilty until proven innocent. You might suggest a play or an idea to a coach, and it gets shot down right away, like: 'Your idea is no good because I didn't think of it.' But if you do that too often, people stop coming up with ideas. And then you might be shutting off the flow of pretty good thoughts, and you're stunting everyone's development. I don't want to be dictating. I want to be having conversations.* [20]

So remember the rule for generating new and creative ideas: first, get all the possibilities on the table; then, you can go back and compare and evaluate them, hunting for the winning ideas in the bunch.

Silence Can Be Golden

One of the biggest adjustments for new coaches is getting used to the silence that follows a curious or powerful question. It can be quite unnerving. Our own internal dialogue fills in the silence with anxious thoughts about what the other person may be thinking – especially about us and our approach to the conversation. We might also worry that their silence means they've checked out of the conversation, or they're not interested. The temptation is to jump in and ask another question, interject a witty comment or offer an insightful observation.

In reality, what's usually going on in the other person's mind is some interesting thinking. It takes a lot more thought to respond to a curious or powerful question than a "yes" or "no" type question. When people are engaged in developing new perspectives, they often need more time to sift through their ideas and process their thoughts. When we rush to fill the silence – to deal with our own discomfort – we often interrupt the very thing we're trying to evoke through coaching: creative and resourceful thinking.

Our task and challenge as coaches is to manage our own discomfort with silence so that our employee can reap the benefit of the thinking we've helped open up for them.

In the next chapter, we'll explore how the next skill – Open Listening – allows us to harvest the fruit of our Curious Questioning. Our questions are only effective if we are open in our listening as well.

What to Take Away from This Chapter

- Genuine curiosity makes the difference between your employee feeling comfortable enough to share their thoughts and feelings, as opposed to feeling interrogated, diagnosed or judged.

- Powerful questions are short, simple, open-ended (requiring more than a "yes" or "no" response), and don't have a "right" answer. They cause people to think more deeply and creatively. They usually start with "What" or "How" (rather than "Why" which can provoke defensiveness).

- Curious questions are a powerful tool for uncovering different perspectives: what do others think? What possibilities do we see if we look at the situation from different angles?

- Curious questions can also be used to generate new and creative ideas. The key as a manager-coach is to create a safe space for innovative thinking to take root. Brainstorm first, evaluate later.

- New coaches need to get used to the unnerving silence that follows a curious or powerful question, since this is when the employee is doing the very thing we're trying to evoke through coaching: creative and resourceful thinking.

"A committed listener helps people think more clearly, work through unresolved issues, and discover the solutions they have inside them."

- Robert Hargrove

Chapter 7

Skill #3:
Open Listening

It may seem self-evident that listening well is an essential component of good leadership and at the heart of exceptional coaching. Yet in a fast paced working environment, Open Listening has become quite rare. Mastering it is an acquired skill that comes through frequent use, especially when under pressure to produce results.

Listening is a big topic – and possibly the most crucial coaching skill. That's one of the reasons this chapter is the longest of all the ones focusing on the core Coaching for Engagement™ skills. Here's how we'll walk through the subject:

- What is Open Listening?

- What is it like to be heard when someone listens to us openly?

- What are the benefits of investing in Open Listening – even though it takes time, energy, concentration and patience?

- What does stress do to the quality of our listening – and how can we counteract that effect?

- What are some of the fundamentals of Open Listening?

- Building on the fundamentals, how can we listen in four dimensions (listening at a physical, emotional, mental and 'spiritual' level)?

We'll close the chapter by looking at some of the common pitfalls of Open Listening and how we can avoid them.

Listening With More Than Our Ears, Hearing More Than Words

When we delivered our first Coaching for Engagement™ program in China, as part of the preparation for the session, we discovered the characters that make up the verb "to listen" in Cantonese denote something significant about

EAR

EYES

UNDIVIDED
ATTENTION

HEART

this skill.

The word (roughly pronounced in English as "ting") means pay close attention – with our ears, eyes, and a focused heart – to the sounds, tones, and gestures of the speaker. This more holistic approach to listening includes hearing not only words, but also the full meaning and emotion behind them. That means we use our ears, eyes, and heart when listening while giving our undivided attention. If we want to coach well, we need to tune our "antennae" so we're listening with more than just our ears, and hearing more than just words.

The Experience of Being Heard

Being seen, heard, and understood are fundamental needs of all human beings. When was the last time you felt truly heard and understood? One of the most powerful insights participants in Coaching for Engagement™ programs experience is the opportunity to be listened to in a whole new way. Once managers get a taste of what it means to be listened to openly, they often can't wait to give the same gift to others.

Here's what Gail Pickard, a senior manager at a large insurance corporation in Canada had to say about Open Listening and the experience of being heard:

> *Active listening includes not just what's being said, but what's unsaid and what's behind what's being said. [When you are listening to me as a coach] you hear the subtext or see the underlying theme and will articulate it when sometimes I may be having trouble doing that.*[21]

To start practicing this skill right away, try out Exercise 2.

Exercise 2: Opening Up Your Listening

The next time someone comes to you with an issue they would like some input on, in a calm voice, ask them the following question: "Describe the problem in 25 words or less... what is the issue."

The request doesn't imply judgment but simply a request for the person to be succinct in their thinking and speaking.

It may take them a moment to process their thoughts before responding. Give them that space. Let them know you are listening. Use this moment to focus on your intent to really listen to what you are hearing – not with the intent to solve it for them, but to ensure you hear what they are communicating to you. Nothing more.

The goal is not to solve, but to just listen.

Sidebar 1: The power of being heard

Creating a safe environment for employees to speak up in Chinese business culture

Weiliang Le, Managing Director of SAP Business Objects' Development Center in Shanghai, has this to say about the particular impact and importance of coaching skills like Open Listening in China:

"Because of the culture, people are more shy to talk and to express their opinions in China. By using curious questions, you are forcing them to speak their opinion. In China, people tend to hide their feelings in their hearts; if you use curious questions and Open Listening, it helps them speak out. Because of the culture, it is harder and riskier [for managers] to practice as a coach, but even more important than in Western countries."[22]

Creating the right environment for candid conversation has shifted the culture in some organizations in China. Some companies now *"encourage one-on-one meetings between management and employees, in which employees have a chance to air their opinions to senior managers privately. This practice suits the Chinese culture well because Chinese generally feel much more comfortable speaking their minds on a one-on-one basis... it also encourages its employees to take risks for new ideas and allows them to make mistakes without fear of punishment."*[23]

There is power in listening. When we do it well, we provide an opportunity for others to voice what is on their mind (and hearts) and to open up to new possibilities.

Slowing Down to Speed Up: How Open Listening Pays Off

When you engage in Curious Questioning and Open Listening, it may feel like you're spending more time on the issue than you need to. That's partly true – but you're making an investment that pays off over time. Let's explore why it works – and why it's worth it. First, let's look at what the other person feels if you truly listen openly:

- They feel understood.
- They feel their thoughts and perspectives are valued.

- They feel more confident and comfortable sharing important information with you.

- They feel more calm (having the opportunity to voice what is on their mind can help diffuse any negative energy associated with it).

They are then ready to move forward and explore next steps or new possibilities, because they reach a state where they are more effectively engaged in finding a resourceful way to address their issue. This is how the time and energy you invest in Open Listening begins to pay off. Your listening creates the environment for people to re-engage. The benefits of that are twofold. First, you avoid the experience of having "repeat" conversations with your employee down the road. Open Listening is a key ingredient that allows the employee to truly move forward in their thinking so they don't stay stuck or circle back to the same problem. Second, continuing to listen openly instead of offering advice – even when it requires a lot of energy and patience – helps your employee stay responsible for solving their own problem.

Using Open Listening and the broader coaching process empowers employees, equipping them with the thinking space and skills to solve their own problems. Ultimately, that saves you time, and yields better results. It's also a good way to ensure you keep the monkey (other people's challenges) on their back, and not let it jump onto yours. You've got enough monkeys on your own back!

In a recent interview, Thomas Guerrero, a director in a provincial health ministry, shared his perspective on Open Listening, and the impact that it has had on his relationship with his staff:

> *If you go into a conversation knowing beforehand [exactly] what you want to get out of it and where you want it to go, people tend to feel a little bit dejected ... [but] if you go into a conversation with an open mind and allow employees to speak freely and then formulate your questions and ideas based on*

what they're saying to you, not only do they feel more valued because they're hearing you repeat back to them what they just said, but you're going to come up with a better outcome from the conversation...I tried to listen before, but I really do pay attention better now and it has improved my relationship with my staff...[I think now] people are more open about coming to talk to me about things.[24]

Listening Is a Challenge When We Feel Stressed and Pressed for Time or Results

If you're like us, you may listen well sometimes, but not nearly as well when you're stressed and pressed for time or results. We all feel time pressure as managers, whether our own, or that of others who bring their urgent problems to us. Put another way, people don't often want to learn how to fish, they just want the fish. Giving answers yields the desired short-term results, but by doing so, we miss an opportunity to foster long-term development. We need to not only generate performance in the moment, but also build capacity for the future.

Here's what happens to our listening when we're under stress. You'll remember in Chapter 5 we talked about energy management. Stress affects all four elements of our energy. Physically and emotionally, we drift into the "survival mode" quadrants (Figure 4 in Chapter 5), and mentally, our more resourceful and creative thinking shuts down. 'Spiritually', we may lose sight of our best intentions for the conversation. As a result, our listening degrades into "listening to respond."[25] Rather than listening to understand, we listen merely waiting for openings to advocate or argue our own point of view or solution.

Our observation is that without feedback and positive reinforcement around the value of listening, even seasoned leaders tend to do a lot more telling than asking – especially under stress. Our guess is that it's perhaps a reflection of their "busyness" as well as their accumulated experience; people who have advanced up the corporate ladder like to rely on the strengths that got them there (which likely included having a ready answer or solution).

How can you counteract the effect of stress and pressure on your listening? If you're heading into a coaching conversation, here are a couple of things you can do to help open up your listening again:

- Remember what it feels like to be truly listened to. When was the last time you were truly listened to you? Who did the listening? How did they do that? What was the effect for you? Being heard is one of the great gifts that we can give to each other at no cost.

- Revisit some of the tips in Chapter 5 for managing your energy both before and during a conversation.

Fundamentals of Open Listening

Let's get more specific about what Open Listening looks like in action. One of the best ways to do that is to compare and contrast it with closed listening.

Closed Listening occurs when we hear the words of the other person but focus in on what the message means to *us*. In Closed Listening the spotlight is on me – my own thoughts, judgments, opinions, and feelings. We may be smiling and nodding, but the dialogue we are paying attention to is our own internal dialogue. We listen to the other individual superficially and hear only passively.

Some of the questions that might pass through our mind when we're in a closed listening mode include:

- "How is this going to impact **me**?"

- "When have **I** experienced this in the past too?"

- "What would **I** do about this?"

- "Where could **I** take this conversation next?"

- "What do **I** need to tell them?"

- "When can **I** get my example in?"

- "Yeah, but **I** have a better example of that to share…"

If these sound a little too familiar, don't worry – most of us naturally operate at this level most of the time – there's no need to beat yourself up about it. The only problem is, closed listening prevents deeper levels of connection, awareness and understanding from surfacing – largely because it fails to make the speaker feel heard and valued. It also tends to go hand in hand with falling into teaching or telling mode, rather than remaining present and open.

In contrast, **Open Listening** is focused completely on the other person, the topic of greatest concern to her/him, and their thought process and feelings. Our awareness is totally centered on the other person's insights, development and results. It involves listening for their words, expressions, emotions, everything they bring to the conversation. When you're doing this well, you notice what they say, how they say it, and even what they don't say. You're listening for their values, frames of reference, and any feelings being expressed. In short, you're listening to the whole person, not just their words.

Some questions we can ask ourselves to keep our focus internally when practicing Open Listening include:

- "What are **they** focused on?"

- "What does this mean for **them**?"

- "How are **they** measuring success here?"

- "What values are **they** expressing under their words?"

- "What emotions am I noticing in **their** voice?"

- "What underlying beliefs or assumptions could **they** be expressing?"

- "How is this impacting **them** right now?"

- "What strengths have **they** articulated that could be acknowledged?"

- "What are **they** really asking for?"

Sound tiring to keep the focus on them? It can be. Listening in this way requires an enormous amount of concentration and energy. But as with any under-used muscle, it gets easier and more natural with use. And the return on the investment of your energy – in terms of your employee's engagement – makes it well worth the effort.

Listening To the Whole Person: Four-Dimensional Listening

In the previous section, we looked at the fundamentals of Open Listening – placing our focus on the other person. Building on that foundation, how do we then expand and broaden our focus to listen to them as a whole person? How do we make sure that we understand the full message they're trying to communicate to us – including not only their words, but also the full meaning and feeling behind them?

In previous chapters, we've talked about the four kinds of energy that we all carry with us: physical, emotional, mental, and spiritual. We've found that paying attention at each of these levels is helpful when we're listening. Listening through each filter or lens provides us with important information and clues about the underlying context that shapes people's perceptions and behaviour. We call it four-dimensional listening.

So what do you listen for in each dimension? Table 10 provides a quick overview.

Table 10: Overview of Four-Dimensional Listening

Dimension	Focus	What to Observe or Sample Questions to Ask to Deepen Listening
Physical	Non-verbal communication (body language)	Observe eye movement, sitting position, facial expressions, gestures, breathing patterns. Check out any assumptions made based on body language: "I'm sensing _____. Is that an accurate reflection of what you feel/think/believe?"
Emotional	Feelings and emotions	What's your initial feeling about the situation? What's your reaction to all this? What's most _____ (challenging, energizing, interesting, disturbing, concerning, frustrating) about the situation? What part of the situation frustrates you right now? What part of it excites you? Overall, which way is the scale tipping – toward frustration or excitement? On a scale of 1 to 10, how _____ (concerned, optimistic, angry) are you about this?
Mental	Thinking process and mental models	If you were standing on the sidelines of this situation, what would you see? How would you describe it to someone? If this situation was a scene from a sports game, what would it be? Who is the hero, the victim and the villain in this situation? If you were to zoom out and see the situation from above, what does it look like? Where are things moving and where are they stuck? What else do you notice? If you had to sum up the situation in one word, what would it be? What makes that word so fitting/appropriate?
Spiritual	Values, beliefs, purpose	What is/was so significant and important about that for you?

Next, let's walk through each dimension in more detail.

1. **Physical – listening for non-verbal communication.** There have been a number of helpful books written in recent years about the role of body language in communication. This includes eye movement, sitting position, facial expressions, gestures, and breathing patterns. All of these factors can provide insight into what lies underneath the words being expressed.

   But as with anything we notice about someone in a conversation, we need to be careful about the conclusions we draw. For instance, just because someone crossed their arms or legs, it does not mean that they are feeling threatened, defensive or resistive in the conversation. One helpful phrase for checking out any assumption we might make based on our observation of body language is: *"I'm sensing _____. Is that an accurate reflection of what you feel/think/believe?"*

   What we "hear" at the physical level can help us deepen our listening at the next three levels. For example, language, tone, and body language can all provide a glimpse into the way an individual feels about what you are discussing.

2. **Emotional – listening for feelings and emotions.** We often devalue the importance of feelings and emotions in the workplace, but they impact everything we do. We typically dismiss them when they are positive, only noticing when they become negative.

   When it comes to engagement, the role of our emotions expressed through feelings plays a significant role. When we feel threatened or unsupported, we operate out of survival mode and frame situations differently than when operating out of a sense of opportunity. Putting feelings into words can begin to diffuse the feelings and lower our stress about the situation. One of the gifts we can give someone as a coach is to help them name their experience.

   Here is a short list of feelings we often experience at work:

Angry	Hopeful	Sad
Anxious	Passionate	Exhausted
Challenged	Compassionate	Energized
Fearful	Relaxed	Defensive

Obviously, we would like to help people shift their emotional state from a negative one to a positive one. But first, people often need a chance to express their initial feeling about a situation before they can reframe it. Here are some questions you could ask to help people name their emotional state:

- "What's your initial feeling about the situation?"

- "What's your reaction to all this?"

- "What's most _____ (challenging, energizing, etc.) about this situation for you?"

- "It sounds like you're _____ about the situation – is that true?"

- "What part of the situation frustrates you right now? What part of it excites you?"

- "On a scale of 1 to 10, how _____ (excited, frustrated, optimistic, angry, etc.) are you about this?"

Once they have given voice to their feelings about the situation, they will be in a better place to explore reframing, which you can encourage with some of the questions we look at next in the mental dimension.

3. **Mental – listening for thinking process and mental models.** What's critical here is not just listening to understand the issue or challenge the employee puts on the table, but paying attention to the thought process and mental models they are using to address it. Think of a mental model as a person's story or explanation about how something works, based on their past observations and experience and the assumptions they've made as a result. Remember, your role is not to fix the problem or find

the solution for them. It's to help them clear the obstacles in their own thinking process so they can do it themselves.

One way to hear more at this level is to pay attention to the metaphors individuals use to describe the situation or opportunity before them. For example, you could ask: "How do you see your world at work right now?" Metaphors help us simplify what things mean to us. Using their metaphors as you continue to engage in the conversation will communicate that you understand where they are coming from. Use their words and their language whenever you can.

What we're listening for here is their frame of reference, the set of assumptions that shape their view of the situation. For example, people will make assumptions about the impact of an impending change that will shape whether they see it as a threat or an opportunity. That's their mental model of the change.

Here are some other examples of questions we can use to get a better picture of someone's mental model:

- "If you were standing on the sidelines of this situation, what would you see? How would you describe it to someone?"

- "If this situation were a scene from a sports game, what would it be?"

- "Who is the hero, the victim and the villain in this situation?"

- "If you were to zoom out and see the situation from above, what would it look like? Where are things moving and where are they stuck? What else do you notice?"

- "If you had to sum up the situation in one word, what would it be? What makes that word so fitting/appropriate?"

- "If you were wearing a different hat in the situation (for example, if you were one of the other key players, like a stakeholder, a customer, another employee, one of your peers, etc.), what would you see differently?"

Asking these kinds of questions actually sets employees on the path to reframing their perspective, because they start to view the situation from different angles.

4. **Spiritual – listening for values, beliefs, and purpose.** Whether we are conscious of them or not, we all have values that guide the decisions we make and how we act in the workplace. Uncovering and understanding our employees' values through coaching provides an opportunity to help them connect their work with what matters most to them. When they can align the focus of their work and their day-to-day choices and behaviours with their deepest values, their level of engagement and motivation will rise.

    Two people could be doing the same task or pursuing the same goal, with completely different values motivating them. For instance, someone may be eager to complete a project on time out of a sense of loyalty to the individual they are working for, while another may be doing it to feed their desire to achieve.

    A more extensive list of commonly held values is provided in the resource section of our website (www.coachingforengagement.com) , but here are a few values we often hear expressed by clients in conversations:

Directness	Accomplishment	Contribution
Honesty	Integrity	Excellence
Accuracy	Creativity	Focus
Growth	Authenticity	Harmony
Collaboration	Inspiration	Trust
Joy	Risk-taking	Innovation

One very simple way to uncover what someone values is to simply ask why something is important or significant to them. Since "why" questions can often put people on the defensive, another way of asking the same thing is to say: *What is/was so significant and important about that for you?* Be sure to ask it in a curious, open way – not an interrogative way. How something is expressed can make all the difference.

If you are interested in a quick way to identify some of your own core values, try Exercise 3 below.

Exercise 3: Clarifying Your Own Values

Think back over the past six months and pick out one thing that you have accomplished that you are really proud of. It can be personal or professional. Got something in mind?

Now ask yourself, "What was significant about that accomplishment for me?"

Write down your thoughts.

Then ask yourself, "What is important about that for me?"

The answer may not come as easily this time – that's a good sign because it means you are digging deeper.

If you ask yourself the question up to five times, you should be able to get down to one or more of your values at work.

By paying attention to all four dimensions of an individual – and rotating our focus among them – we notice the threads connecting non-verbal signals (physical), feelings (emotional), thoughts (mental), values and beliefs ('spiritual'). When we tune in and absorb this wealth of information about the individual, we are better equipped to come with questions to ask next to help move them from insight to engagement. There is a lot to listen to with just one other person in the room – more than we can focus on at any point in time – which explains why really listening can be so exhausting!

Common Pitfalls on the Road to Open Listening

Giving someone our complete focus, keeping it there and practicing four-dimensional listening takes more than just eliminating distractions. It requires a genuine interest and curiosity about the other individual. It also means doing your best to steer away from thinking traps that can pull you out of Open Listening. Here are the most common pitfalls you need to watch out for:

1. **Solving the wrong problem.** When you coach, there is always a creative tension between wanting to reach an outcome versus just listening. If you rush and try to move the employee to the point of taking action or generating solutions before listening enough, it's easy to fall into the trap of solving the wrong problem – the surface issue, rather than the underlying issue. Open Listening ensures you see the big picture, so you can be sure you're addressing the right problem or opportunity.

2. **Getting caught up in the manager agenda (losing the balance with the coach agenda).** It's difficult to remain open and curious when someone's performance (or lack thereof) impacts your own objectives. In Chapter 2, we talked about the manager-coach's challenge of wearing two hats and balancing two agendas: the employee's performance (manager hat) and the employee's development (coach hat). Ultimately your role as a manager is to cultivate high performance and results. Your role as a coach in the conversation is to stay open to how those results are achieved and support the long-term development of the individual. Sometimes articulating the challenge of balancing the two agendas, and including your employee in finding solutions that can both improve performance and generate development, can be helpful in freeing up your listening again.

3. **Jumping to the rescue.** As leaders, you are often looked to and expected to have answers. You justifiably take great pride in your ability to analyze situations and provide solutions. As a result, one of the biggest temptations for you as a coach will be jumping in with your own solutions and advice because you believe that is what people expect of you. But if you do that, you take away an opportunity for the individual to cultivate their own solutions and learn how to address similar issues in the future. When you feel the urge to speak ask yourself, *"Why am I about to give advice before attempting to understand this person?"*

Sometimes the temptation to jump in is driven less by the belief about what people expect of us, and more by the desire to rescue someone from the discomfort of wrestling with their thoughts and their situation. The need to alleviate tension can sometimes override the need to just be present and to let an individual work things through and articulate their thoughts clearly. If that sounds familiar to you, ask yourself, *"Is the question I am about to ask serving my needs or theirs?"* Remember: sometimes the greatest gift you can give as a coach is silence, providing space for the other person to arrive at key insights.

4. **Assumptions, beliefs, and judgments.** As you listen to someone, part of your brain will be busy deciding whether you agree or disagree with what they are saying, based on your own assumptions, values and beliefs. Some of what they say may also trigger either judgments or defensiveness for you. As soon as that happens, you're in closed listening. Recognize when this happens, and gently recommit to shifting your focus back to trying to fully understand what is being communicated, not how it affects you.

5. **Getting caught up in the story (details).** Sometimes you will get so caught up in someone's story – the drama or the details – that you will lose sight of the goal of the coaching conversation. Your role is not to dig out all the information and facts in order to diagnose and prescribe a solution. While the story content may be interesting, great coaches are focused on what's behind the story. Questions that you might ask as a coach to pull someone out of the details and back to the picture could be: *"From your perspective, what's the most important thing about what happened (or is happening)?"* or *"What's important to you about that story?"*

6. **Discomfort with silence.** If coaching is about helping someone to uncover a new perspective, then silence is providing the space for insights to emerge. Let silence do its work. One way to catch yourself is with this simple word and acronym: W.A.I.T. = Why Am I Talking?

In the next chapter, we'll explore how Curious Questioning (Skill #2) and Open Listening (Skill #3) blend into Appreciative Discovery (Skill #4), allowing you to engage employees in identifying and channelling their strengths.

What to Take Away from This Chapter

- Open Listening involves paying close attention and hearing more than the words that are being spoken.

- Stay completely focused on the other person, on the topic of greatest concern to them, and on their thought process.

- Keep your awareness centered on the other person's insights, development and results.

- Focus on all four dimensions of the other person's energy: watch their body language and tone of voice (physical energy) for clues about what to listen for at other levels; ask about their feelings and reactions (emotional energy); inquire about their assumptions, thinking process, and perspective (mental energy); identify deeply held values and beliefs that motivate them most powerfully ('spiritual' energy).

"The deepest principle of human nature is the craving to be appreciated."

- William James

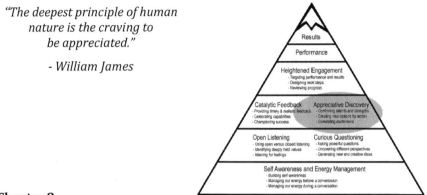

Chapter 8

Skill #4: Appreciative Discovery

One of the signs of great managers is that they can describe, in detail, the unique talents of each of their people – what drives each one, how each one thinks, how each builds relationships. Their goal is to help each individual contribute his or her best to the common goal. It's the perspective that a manager takes – the perspective of appreciation – that enables their direct reports to shine in their roles. At its core, Appreciative Discovery is the search for the strengths and most positive attributes in each of your employees. It is also the exploration of how your employees can better channel those strengths toward the team's and the organization's goals.

In this chapter, we'll explore three aspects of the acquired skill of Appreciative Discovery:

- *Confirming talents and strengths* by looking for others' unique capacities and genius

- *Creating new options for action* by looking for opportunities to focus your employee's talent and motivation

- *Generating excitement about positive possibilities* by focusing on potential solutions rather than problems.

You'll notice we called this an acquired skill. That's because, unfortunately, our brain unwittingly tends to do the opposite. We have a strong pull to focus on the negative, on the problem, on what's wrong, on why things can't work or won't work. Our brains are wired to scan constantly for challenges, danger or negative feedback much more effectively than they are to notice what is going well. It's a survival mechanism that has served us well for centuries, but can get in the way of developing our fullest potential and that of the person we're coaching. That's why Appreciative Discovery takes conscious effort on our part, to counteract our natural tendency to focus on problems instead of possibilities.

Like many other consultants who work in the field of organizational effectiveness, whenever we do employee focus groups, a consistent theme emerges – people are not thanked and acknowledged for their contributions nearly enough. Without sincere appreciation, creating engagement is impossible. Positive reinforcement invites people to contribute their talents and passion.

What happens when we are more appreciative of others' talents, strengths and ideas? In a lot of cases, employees are surprised initially! After that, it puts them far more at ease in a conversation: it feels good to be recognized and seen. This is not about blowing sunshine up people's proverbial backsides. It needs to be grounded in truth, not something we manufacture to make them feel better about themselves. To start putting this into action, try Exercise 4.

Exercise 4: Pure and Simple Appreciation

For the next week, when you are in conversations with your employees, ONLY mention their strengths and positive things that you notice them doing.

Make no attempt to add mention of their weaknesses – or even to compare and contrast their current performance to previous (weaker) performance.

Notice what happens when you focus only on the positive. How do you feel? How does your perception of your employees change?

Notice how your employees behave as a result. Maybe they are taking more pride in their work? Taking more initiative? Tackling tasks more enthusiastically? Behaving more positively during your interactions?

Sidebar 2: The Roots of Appreciative Discovery

There are two parts to Appreciative Discovery. The first is adopting an appreciative perspective, recognizing and valuing the positive contributions and qualities of people around us. The second is becoming an explorer, open to discovering new possibilities. By appreciating what is good and valuable in the present situations, we can discover how to build on it moving forward.

Appreciative Discovery has its roots in two schools of thought or approaches that have started to gain a foothold in organizational life in recent years.

1. **Appreciative Inquiry**[26] (AI) is a process (and underlying philosophy) that involves individuals throughout an organization in its renewal, change and performance. AI is based on the assumption that we create more of whatever we focus on. The focus that an organization holds – and the way it asks questions of itself – will determine the way it evolves and changes over time. If an organization continually focuses on problems or difficult situations (by asking *"What problems are we having, and why are we having them?"*), it will keep finding more of the same. If the same organization tries to appreciate what is best in itself (by asking *"What is working well around here, and how are we making that happen?"*), it will find/discover more and more of what is good.

2. **Strengths-based management and leadership** is based on the idea that each person should focus on – and work in – their strength areas on a daily basis and merely "manage" their weaknesses instead of trying to fix them (by trying to become "well-rounded"). This notion was popularized in Marcus Buckingham's books *"First, Break All the Rules"* and *"Now, Manage Your Strengths"* and has been advanced through further research by The Gallup Organization. They have found that people have several times more potential for growth when they invest energy in developing their strengths instead of correcting their deficiencies. Their studies indicate that:

    *   *People who have the opportunity to focus on their strengths every day are six times as likely to be engaged in their jobs and more than three times as likely to report having an excellent quality of life in general.*[27]

    *   *If a manager focuses primarily on their employees' strengths, their employees have only a 1% chance of being actively disengaged. If he or she focuses primarily on their employees' weaknesses, those employees have a 22% chance of being actively disengaged. If a manager primarily ignores their employees, their employees have a 40% probability of being actively disengaged.*[28]

    *   *In organizations where leadership focuses on strengths, employees have a 73% probability of being engaged at work. By contrast, in organizations where leadership does not focus on strengths, employees have only a 9% chance of being engaged at work.*[29]

Confirming Talents and Strengths

The intent of Appreciative Discovery is to uncover what someone is already doing well, with the intent of leveraging that success. The idea is to use questions, observations and suggestions to shine a spotlight on your employees' abilities, talents, interests, experience and unique qualities. Then you can pick up on – and reinforce – the points of real passion and engagement.

In addition to using your powers of observation, you can also use some of the curious questions in Box 7 to uncover the unique brilliance of your employees. By brilliance, we mean the unique talents and other strengths the person contributes to the workplace.

Box 7: Questions for Discovering More About Your Employees' Talents, Strengths, Interests and Preferred Methods of Recognition

What are you most excited or passionate about in your work right now? Or, what would get you more excited and passionate about your work?

What's the work that has been most enjoyable for you in the last three months? Or, what was the best day at work you've had in the last 3 months? What were you doing? What made it so enjoyable? What skills and abilities were you using?

What are you really proud of accomplishing in the past six months? What talents did you bring to bear on that task?

What are you really good at?

How have you contributed to ... ?

What was the best recognition you ever received? What made it so great? How else do you like to be recognized?

How do you like to learn new things? What would you like to learn more about? What really grabs your interest?

We often need to remind and reinforce employees that they have strengths that can be built on when they face new or challenging situations. As a manager, you want to help them become more aware of – and take greater ownership of – the unique brilliance that you appreciate the most in them.

Creating New Options for Action

Once you and your employee share a better understanding of their strengths, talents, and interests, you're in a much better position to explore opportunities to channel those to achieve the organization's goals and the employee's own development goals.

Here are some of the coaching questions we can ask to help our employees create new options for action:

- "What are the possibilities that you see for using more of your strengths every day?"

- "How could you use your talents and strengths in an even better way for yourself and the organization?"

- "Since you're good at _____, what could you contribute to Project _____ if we included you on the team?"

- "If you were to play a different role than you usually do on an upcoming project (a role that really plays to your strengths), what would be one possibility? How about another?"

- "What other possibilities do you see now that you didn't see before?"

At Atlassian Software Company, once a month, they tell employees that for the next 24 hours, they can work on whatever they want, in whatever way they want, with whomever they want (as long as they share their ideas and any tangible progress they achieve).[30]   As a way of stretching your employees' imagination, you could ask them: *"If we gave you that same opportunity, what would you do?"* You could follow up on their answer by asking: *"What do you think would be most interesting and enjoyable for you about that? What would be the benefit to the organization?"* The goal is to get the creative thinking wheels turning.

Generating Excitement about Positive Possibilities

The quickest way to generate excitement that will translate into an employee taking action is to help them find a connection between those options and their intrinsic motivators. In his book *"Drive: The Surprising Truth About What Motivates Us,"* Daniel Pink identifies three elements of true motivation: *autonomy* (the desire to direct our own work, including what we do, how we do it, when we do it, and who we do it with), *mastery* (the desire to learn and create new things), and *purpose* (the desire to make a difference and leave the world a better place). You don't necessarily need to know which of these generates the most excitement for a particular employee in order to tell if they've tapped into a core motivator because you'll be able to see it in their body language: their face and speech may become more animated, their eyes may look brighter, they may use more hand gestures and sit up straighter.

Here are some of the questions you can ask to generate excitement about new possibilities:

- "Of all the options we've talked about, which one excites/interests you most? Which one do you feel most motivated to work on?"
- "What excites/interests you most about that opportunity?"
- "What would be the best part about it for you?"
- "What would succeeding at that give you?"
- "What would achieving that get you?"

As they are coming up with new options for action (or reviewing them to try and choose one), watch their body language closely to gauge which options are fuelled by true motivation. Those are the options worthy of more discussion and follow through.

In Closing

Rob Eisses, former CEO of Icron, shared these thoughts on how the process of Appreciative Discovery plays out over time:

> *You have to probe to figure out what makes somebody tick and then nourish that and help them realize that they are good at something and let them run with it. It is a process that has to be developed over time. It is not an overnight thing, as if a couple of coaching sessions will be enough to get somebody good to go. It's the lifelong learning process and this is just one step on the journey. It's so helpful ... for the individual that is being coached ... to understand their position better and how to make a company more effective – which is the big goal.*[31]

One question that may have entered your mind as we explored the skill of Appreciative Discovery is this: while it's great to focus on the positives, don't we also need to offer our employees feedback on areas for improvement? Absolutely, yes. We'll address that in the next chapter on Catalytic Feedback. The reason we encourage you to focus on Appreciative Discovery first with your employees is this. If the only attention that we give to our growth and development is in the areas of weakness (which is what most of us already do by habit), we may neglect enhancing the areas that made us great to start with. It's much easier – and more fruitful – to build on strengths and unleash more of who we are – than it is to try to be someone we're not for the sake of addressing a weakness.

What to Take Away from This Chapter

- Appreciative Discovery is the search for the strengths and most positive attributes in each of your employees, and an exploration of how to better leverage those.

- Start by confirming the talents and strengths of your employees, combining your own observations of them to date, with what you learn through Curious Questioning.

- Once you and your employee share a better understanding of their strengths, talents, and interests, you're in a much better position to explore opportunities to channel those to advance both the organization's goals and the employee's own development goals (using Curious Questioning to generate options).

- You can generate excitement about specific possibilities for an employee to use their strengths more often by helping them find a connection between those options and what truly motivates them (e.g., getting to shape the way they do a job, getting to learn and create new things, or making a real impact and difference).

"Feedback is one of the most critical requirements for sustained high-level performance of any human act. Without frequent and specific feedback, performance varies and often fails."

- Ferdinand F. Fournies

Chapter 9

Skill #5: Catalytic Feedback

Like all cartoons, the reason this one makes us laugh is because there's truth to it, even if it's exaggerated. In this case, the two truths are: first, that our employees are actually hungry for frequent, specific, useful feedback; and second, that most of the feedback they get from managers tends to be negative, vague and critical (even when it's labelled "constructive").

Catalytic Feedback – whether it's about good or poor performance – helps us learn from experience. When it's delivered with positive intent and received in that spirit, feedback helps us to shape a more accurate perception of our performance – and gives us valuable information we can use to fine-tune or adjust accordingly. That's where the "catalytic" piece comes in. You may or may not remember this from high school chemistry: a catalyst not only speeds up a chemical reaction but it can also help an engine burn cleaner. Feedback should do the same.

In this chapter, we'll discuss:

- The true goal of coaching around feedback (facilitating learning from experience)

- The impact coaching can have on transforming tough feedback into greater engagement

- When to use a coaching style for giving feedback

- How to provide timely and realistic feedback

- How to create successful feedback experiences when performance needs to improve

- How to give feedback that celebrates capabilities (catch someone doing something right and reinforce it with praise)

- How to balance positive and negative feedback

- How to champion successes (help employees set small, high leverage goals that have a good chance of being achieved).

We'll close by looking at the important skill of giving "feedback on the spot."

True Goal of Coaching Around Feedback: Learning from Experience

Before we dive into the specifics, it's important to clarify the purpose of coaching around feedback. For a manager-coach, the goal is twofold: to help the other person learn what to do to improve (how to do it better next time), and to leave them motivated to improve (to want to try to do it better next time). The intent is not to focus on what went wrong this time, but rather to point the direction toward improvement.

You'll notice we used the expression "coaching around feedback" instead of "giving feedback." That's because when it comes to helping an employee learn from experience, your role as a manager-coach will not always be to personally provide feedback. Sometimes it will be, but at other times it will be to help your employee make sense of feedback they've received from others, or to build on their own self-assessment (feedback from themselves).

In this chapter, while we do talk about specific ways for you to give feedback effectively, we are really outlining a coaching approach to helping employees learn from experience and improve their performance.

Next, we'd like to share a story about the catalytic impact that feedback can have, especially when an employee is coached to find practical ways to shift a pattern that's holding them back from being more effective.

Impact of Coaching: Transforming Tough Feedback into Greater Engagement

Years ago we worked with a manager at a manufacturing plant. He was the plant troubleshooter. The feedback he received from a 360-degree survey, completed by people in the plant, revealed he consistently showed up as miserable, angry, and abusive. Brian was his coach.

In the process of one coaching conversation, the manager stated that he didn't quite understand why he had gotten such poor feedback. So Brian inquired curiously, *"Tell me what happens when you get a call about something that has gone wrong."*

He said, "Well, I get the news on my cell phone, usually on the other side of the plant."

"How long does it take you to get to where the problem is?"

"Usually about two or three minutes," he concluded.

"So what do you do with those two or three minutes while you are walking over there?" Brian probed.

There was dead silence for a moment. Then he finally asked, *"What do you mean?"*

"Well, what do you think about when you are walking to the place where the problem is?"

He explained, "Well that's an interesting question. I haven't thought about that before. I just get more and more pissed off trying to figure out who screwed up this time."

The emotion was rich in his voice and body language as he reflected on how situations pushed his hot buttons. Brian went on further, *"What kind of a mood are you in by the time you get to a problem?"*

The manager processed this and stated, "Well... I'm pretty angry! And I usually spend a lot of time blaming so and so for such and such."

In a calm voice, Brian asked, "How else could you spend your time while you walk across the plant?"

The long and the short of the conversation was the manager discovered more positive ways he could focus his thoughts (e.g., on the companies values and how he wanted to interact) and prepare to show up in a more constructive way. What was the impact of that one coaching conversation? Six months later his 360-degree feedback scores and comments reflected a dramatic turn-around.

This story illustrates the impact that feedback can have when we also receive coaching that helps us to make sense of it, and envision ourselves taking practical steps to help us achieve better results.

When to Use a Coaching Approach

As we mentioned earlier, this chapter outlines a coaching approach to helping employees learn from experience and improve their performance. This approach is not necessarily appropriate in all situations. In Chapter 2, we discussed when to use coaching – and when not to. It's important to keep those criteria in mind when you're thinking about offering feedback through coaching.

By way of quick summary, coaching works well with employees who generally display average, good or excellent performance. Coaching can be helpful if: 1) the employee has the skills and ability to complete the task at hand but is struggling with an internal block or external factors impeding their success, 2) they are open to being coached ("coachable"), 3) they are open to being coached by you, and 4) you are not in the midst of a crisis or emergency. In our experience, these conditions are met about 80-90% of the time.

If you are dealing with an employee who is chronically underperforming and/or does not have the prerequisite skills and abilities to do their job (or a particular task), then the ideas and tools in this chapter are not likely to work – they need something different. In all likelihood, you need to adopt a more directive style of leadership and provide them with instruction and close supervision and/or follow the performance management guidelines established by your organization for those situations. If you are looking for more effective ways to provide feedback using a directive style of management, you may want to check out an article called *"The Feedback Sandwich is Out to Lunch"* by Shelle Rose Charvet.[32]

To learn more about our suggested approach for incorporating feedback into your coaching, read on.

Providing Timely and Realistic Feedback

It can surprise us to hear that employees want more feedback, given how uncomfortable it often is both to give and to receive feedback. The reason is our drive to learn and master complex skills runs deep. In order to learn from each experience and move towards mastery, we need feedback – and we know it. At the same time, we're so used to getting negative, unsupportive, ill-timed, or uninvited feedback that we've become reluctant to ask for it and resistant to receiving it. So while an employee may not ask directly for more frequent feedback, they will certainly take the opportunity to make the request indirectly; for example, via an anonymous employee survey (as in the cartoon at the beginning of the chapter).

Consider the story in Box 8. Like the cartoon, it's an exaggeration that contains a truth.

Box 8: Fumbling in the Dark[33]

Picture yourself in a bowling alley, alone, ready to begin a bowling game. Everything seems fine, except, when you release the ball for the first time, the lights go out over the pins. You hear the pins falling but you can't see how many you knocked down.

Looking around you, you see no one, so you yell out, "Hey the lights are out over the pins and I can't see what I knocked down."

A voice replies from somewhere in the area of the pins, *"There are two standing."*

You shout, *"Which two?"*

The voice replies, "Don't bother me. Just bowl again."

Apparently there is no other alternative, so you bowl again toward the pins you cannot see. You don't hear any pins fall. After a moment the lights go on and you see the pins are set up again. So you say to yourself, *"Ah, that's better,"* and you get ready for your second frame.

As you release the ball, the lights over the pins go out again. You yell, *"Hey, how about putting the lights on or teling! me what is going on?"*

You hear the void again say, "Please stop bothering me. I have enough to do back here. Keep bowling. I'll be back in two hours to tell you how you did."

Let's pretend you continue to bowl under those conditions. At the end of two hours, the voice says, *"I'm back."*

You say, "How did I do?"

The voice replies, *"Not too good."*

You say, "What's my score?"

The voice says, "I don't know but it's terrible."

Even if you were a good bowler, that would be no surprise. The reason is that you were deprived of feedback. You were not permitted to see the results of each of your actions and, therefore, you could not make effective corrections in your performance.

Operating without feedback is much like bowling in the dark, especially when it comes to interacting with others. For example, when we have a different working style than another person, we may think we've had a conversation where we successfully knocked down all the pins, but in fact we rolled a gutter ball. Or, when we're told there are still two pins standing but we don't know which ones, it's much like starting a project without sufficient guidance: we don't know where to aim. This is what it's like for your employees: they want to improve their score, and they want you to help shine some light on the situation.

The sooner – and more often – employees get feedback, the sooner they can adjust their behaviour. The more grounded the feedback is in reality, the more helpful it is. Your role as a manager-coach is to provide both timely and realistic feedback. Let's clarify what we mean by both "timely" and "realistic."

Timely Feedback

We usually think of timely meaning as close in time to the event as possible, when the employee's experience is fresh in their mind. This applies equally to both praise and feedback for improvement, allowing us to seize the "teachable moment." When it comes to positive feedback, there is rarely a bad time to offer it – so offer it as frequently as you can do so authentically (i.e., as long as you will mean what you say, and believe the praise is justified).

When it comes to feedback for improvement, you'll need to find a time when an employee is open to receiving the feedback – otherwise it can do more harm than good. That doesn't mean that you can't initiate the conversation or feedback session. The key is to first invite their own self-assessment of their performance, as well as their feelings about it – no matter who initiates the conversation. Listen for any hesitation, uncertainty or defensiveness in their voices. Pick up on their concerns or fears and ask them to elaborate. Notice any negative self-talk. You may find they end up giving themselves the same feedback as you would have.

At this stage, if you feel you have additional feedback to offer that would truly be helpful, first do a quick self-test: *Is this feedback likely to help them improve in their chosen area of growth and development? Is this feedback likely to motivate them to improve?* If you feel comfortable proceeding based on your answers to those two questions, test the waters with them to see if they're open to additional input. If they're not, just let it go for the time being, especially if they're still mired in their emotions about the event and/or feeling extremely self-critical. If they are open to it and you believe your feedback will be helpful, then by all means go ahead, using some of the advice we offer in the next section about how to phrase what you have to say.

Realistic Feedback

This brings us to the content of the feedback you offer. Realistic feedback is simply grounded in reality and our observations. We talk more about how to offer realistic feedback at the positive end of the spectrum in the "Celebrating Capabilities" section later in this chapter. When it comes to feedback for improvement, the closest we can come to reality in our feedback is by offering observations, stripped bare of added judgements and interpretations. Here is a format you can use to phrase feedback as objectively and non-judgementally as possible: *"I notice that when you _____ (observable behaviour without judgemental labels attached), I (or other people) react/respond by _____."* For example:

- "I noticed that when you sped up and started talking more quickly near the end of your presentation, people started to get restless and looked like they had stopped listening."

- "When you were chairing the meeting and did not intervene when Mike was going on at length about Issue X, the rest of the group started to tune out."

- "When I stop by your office to chat for a few minutes and you glance repeatedly at your computer screen, I don't feel like I'm getting your full attention."

- "I noticed that when you continued to offer ideas and suggestions after Susan (a more senior leader) had signalled she wanted to move on, she looked upset/angry/frustrated."

Part of the reason these kinds of observations are effective as feedback is that they tend to evoke less defensiveness since they contain little negative judgement.

In the next section, we look at how to provide timely and realistic feedback to enable an employee to learn from an experience where they did not perform as well as both of you would have liked.

Creating Successful Feedback Experiences When Performance Needs Improvement

When you hear the word "feedback," what do you immediately think of? If you're like most people, it's probably something like: *"Uh-oh, here it comes."* That's because most of us have come to associate feedback with criticism, so we understandably brace ourselves against it. At the same time, we need to be able to learn from experience where we didn't perform the way we'd hoped. If you're going to offer feedback as a manager-coach, you have to find a way to avoid triggering that kind of bracing or defensiveness. That requires a few conditions to be in place. In Table 11 we outline those conditions and suggest practical ways you can help to create them.

Table 11: Creating Successful Feedback Experiences

Conditions for Successful Feedback Experience	Practical Ways You Can Help Create These Conditions as a Manager-Coach
The person must have some self-awareness of the need for improvement in a specific area	Ask them first to share their own self-assessment of their performance: *"How are you feeling about the situation and your role in it?"* Here are the kinds of questions you might ask to guide that interaction: "How did the _____ go (e.g., meeting with client, presentation to committee, etc.)? How do you think you did?" "How are you feeling about it in this moment?" "On a scale of 1-10, how pleased are you with the result? What would a '10' have looked like?" "What do you wish you'd done more of, or less of, in that situation?" "What else did you learn from the experience?" "What are you planning to do next time?" "Is there anything I can do to support you with that?"

The person must be willing to receive feedback <u>from you</u>	Ask: "Are you looking for feedback? Would feedback be helpful?"
	If so, then ask: "What specifically would you like feedback about? What kind of feedback would be helpful right now?"
	Let them dictate the parameters of the feedback they are interested in and willing to receive:
	"So, just to clarify, you'd like to get better at _____ (e.g., delivering presentations, behaving appropriately with senior leaders, etc.). What kind of feedback would you like from me to help with that?"
	"Are you asking me for feedback on how I see you _____?"
The person must trust your intention in giving the feedback	Ask yourself:
	Does the feedback I want to offer serve this person? Is it the kind of feedback they've asked for?
	Am I offering feedback that should be addressed in a performance review discussion?
	If the answer to the first question is that the feedback primarily serves your purpose (i.e., it's not feedback they are inviting or open to receiving right now), or if the answer to the second question is that the feedback you have in mind is something you've avoided giving in performance discussions, then it has no place in a coaching conversation.[34]
The person must trust your feedback is realistic (i.e., sense that there is a kernel of truth in the feedback even if they don't like hearing it)	Listen closely when they offer their own self-assessment of their performance; where appropriate, tie your observations to related observations you heard them make.
	Ensure that the observations you offer as feedback are as factual, objective and non-judgmental as possible. For example: "I noticed that when you sped up and started talking more quickly near the end of your presentation, people started to get restless and looked like they had stopped listening."

In essence, we're suggesting that you do some "asking" before "telling." When you follow these steps, you build on their existing self-awareness about the area for improvement. We're looking for a "window" to talk to them through, instead of breaking down their door.

Next, we look at ways of offering positive feedback that encourages ongoing improvement.

Celebrating Capabilities

Great Catalytic Feedback is also about offering input and suggestions that recognizes success. It accelerates the process of learning for your employee, moving them to an increased awareness of their strengths and how they can apply them. It will often also increase their willingness to take appropriate responsibility for the desired results. Feedback that is both positive and honest is one of the greatest accelerants for progress.

Bob recalls a moment of positive feedback that is still vivid from years ago: "I remember when I was completing my coaching training, one of the instructors came by while we were practicing and said, 'You're pretty good at this.' Something in his tone told me that he really meant it. That training was almost 10 years ago now, and I can still remember that comment." What comment is equally engraved in your memory? My guess is that all of us have at least one we can easily recollect, and perhaps the person who gave it didn't even know the impact they had on us. Regrettably, it's just as likely you can remember comments that tore down your confidence and caused you to question your strengths and abilities.

The best way to give positive feedback is to ground it in truth. Start catching your people doing something right, and reinforce it with honest praise. Here are a couple of practical ways to give feedback which celebrates capabilities:

- **Recognize their past accomplishments.** This means shining a spotlight on something the individual did/does well. You might say:

  "One thing I've noticed that you do well is . . ."

"Something I've noticed that you're exceptionally good at is . . ."

"Great work!! I particularly appreciated the way that you . . ."

- **Acknowledge their character.** This takes note of the character the employee had to demonstrate in order to accomplish a certain action or result. What values or qualities did you see them put into action? You might say:

"I want to acknowledge the initiative it took to confront that conflict directly."

"I want to acknowledge your patience with me."

"I want to acknowledge how resilient you've been despite all the recent changes."

The key, at that point, is to leave them with the encouragement and invitation to do it again by applying it to a current or upcoming challenge. You can easily build on your positive feedback and close with an inquiry such as: *"How could you bring that same _____ (initiative, patience, resilience, etc.) to this situation/project?"*

Balancing Positive and Negative Feedback

Recent research suggests the frequency of small, positive interactions makes a huge difference in ensuring the success of relationships, whether at home or at work. The same research[35] suggests there may be a "magic ratio" in terms of the balance between positive and negative interactions (or positive to negative feedback). It appears the ratios lies somewhere between 3:1 and 13:1 (above that, it has the opposite effect, but there is no need to worry since most of us are not in danger of reaching that upper limit!). Workgroups that reach these ideal ratios are significantly more productive than those who don't.

The implication is you want to have 4 or 5 positive (not just neutral) interactions with your employee for each time you have a negative interaction (e.g., giving feedback that may be hard for them to hear). Keep in mind these can be very short, small interactions – even a positive comment in passing in the hallway, asking how their weekend was, or smiling as you catch their eye across the office or meeting table.

When we talk about this idea of balancing positive and negative interactions and feedback, it can be tempting to want to achieve that balance within a conversation. The "feedback sandwich" technique is one such attempt. You may be familiar with it: the idea is to make a specific positive comment, offer a critique or suggestion for improvement, then close with an overall positive comment, effectively "sandwiching" the negative feedback between two pieces of positive feedback. While the intent is to make negative feedback easier to give and receive, it can also set up an unfortunate association in some people's mind, linking positive and negative feedback Sadly, people begin to brace themselves when they hear praise, wondering what's coming next.

Our suggestion is to separate the two as much as possible. Offer positive feedback in small, frequent doses, and keep it grounded in the truth (i.e., offer it when you mean it). When you have negative feedback to offer, increase your chances of it being received favourably by using the ideas and tools outlined in the *"Creating Successful Feedback Experiences"* section earlier in this chapter.

Next we explore how to help employees translate feedback – whether feedback from you or from themselves – into goals for improvement.

Championing Success: Setting Goals for Improvement

The spirit of this element of Catalytic Feedback is to call forth the champion in each of your employees, helping them achieve more than they initially believe themselves capable of. Your role is to see the positive in an employee, name it, and encourage them to go further with it than they think they can. Ideally, the result is your employees feel more willing to be brave in areas where they previously felt more vulnerable or less confident. *What would it be like if you really believed in your employees' ability to succeed and acted as if they were worth championing?*

At a practical level, this part of the feedback process is about helping your employees set improvement goals that have a good chance of being achieved. Here are some of the kinds of questions you might ask to help them scope appropriate, achievable goals:

- If it's a simple behaviour, you might ask: "What would success look like for you if you did it well next time?"

- If it's a larger improvement they're working on, you might ask: *"What would success look like for you three months from now?"*

- If they're looking for a professional "stretch" but they're not yet sure what it is, you might ask: "If you knew that you couldn't fail, what would you take on? What are you itching to do that would take you beyond your comfort zone?"

Sometimes, an employee will get stuck in their thinking at this stage, believing they are unable to improve. They've developed a story or self-image they have of themselves as "always" doing something wrong (e.g., *"I always lose my confidence around so-and-so"*) or "never" getting something right (e.g., *"I never remember details like that"*). This is why the concept of championing is so important. As a manager-coach, your role in these situations is to remind them of how capable they are. You can do that by helping them hunt for exceptions, or instances when the problem doesn't happen (or only partially). For example, you could ask:[36]

- "Is that true – that you really never/always _____ ?"

- "Can you think of a time when you did/didn't _____ ? What was different about that time?" or, "When is the problem not so bad? If you think of the most recent time the problem didn't happen, what transpired instead?"

- "What do you suppose you did that made the difference? How did you do that?"

Based on what you hear, you can then circle back to the questions of *"what does success look like"* on a specific time frame.

The championing process is also about encouraging and standing up for the employee when they doubt or question their capabilities. You can say things like *"I know you can do it because I've seen you _____ (name one of their accomplishments)"* and *"I know you'll be great at this because one of the things you do well is _____ (name one of their strengths)"* to help bolster their confidence.

Feedback on the Spot

In Chapter 7, we talked about four-dimensional listening, which involves bringing your full attention to the employee during the coaching conversation, observing their physical energy (body language), emotional energy (feelings), mental energy (perspective on the situation), and 'spiritual' energy (values and beliefs). There are times where we can move the conversation forward by sharing what we hear and notice through our four-dimensional listening. For example, we might mirror back to them something they may not be aware of or point out inconsistencies that may need further exploration.

When we do this, we signal that we're open to them bringing their feelings into the conversation. This can be particularly useful in managing the emotional content of the conversation: making sure any negative feelings that could interfere with progress are surfaced, and reflecting back positive feelings so they become more strongly anchored.

Here are a few examples of how you might provide "feedback on the spot":

- Sharing observations about body language and energy, especially a sudden shift: "I noticed your energy really dropped since we got on to this topic – your shoulders slumped and you've been looking down a lot. What is happening for you?" or "I can really see how excited/passionate/interested you are about this project/topic – your whole face changes and you look much more animated."

- Checking out inconsistencies between spoken word and body language: "I'm sensing that you don't feel as enthusiastic about this as your words suggest. Is there any truth to that?" or "You say that you're okay with the situation, but I suspect you do mind more than you're letting on." As always with emotions, we are only guessing what's going on for the other person when we try to interpret how they're feeling based on their body language. The key is to share your guess about what's going on and then ask them to correct you. If you don't want to hazard a guess or put a label on what they might be feeling, you could say something like: "It sounds like you've got mixed/strong feelings about this project/challenge – can you say a bit about that?"

After all that we've talked about with respect to feedback in this chapter, the most important first step you take as a coach – and the one with the biggest impact – may be the simple act of sharing what you notice about your employee's body language, energy level, and emotions. Not only will this help them to feel heard (because you're demonstrating how closely you're listening to them), but it can also help set the tone for conversations, allowing important topics or hidden blocks to surface when they haven't previously.

Some people reading this chapter may think this approach to dealing with feedback seems unnatural. If so, start in small ways that feel comfortable and authentic to you. You may notice this generates the shift and impact you've been looking for in your conversations.

Coming up in the next chapter, we'll talk about how the first four skills we've explored so far in the C.O.A.C.H. approach generates Heightened Engagement – and how to help employees translate that into targeted action to generate performance results for your organization.

What to Take Away from This Chapter

- The twofold purpose of coaching around feedback is to equip and motivate employees to improve. This involves ensuring they figure out *how* to do it better next time, and that they still *want* to improve next time.

- Feedback can have a catalytic impact when an employee is coached to find practical ways to shift a pattern that is holding them back from being more effective.

- Providing feedback as a manager-coach involves building on an employee's existing self-awareness about an area for improvement, much like speaking to them through a window rather than breaking down their door.

- Provide "timely" feedback by doing it as close to the event as possible, while respecting the employee's level of openness to the conversation. Provide "realistic" feedback by offering non-judgemental observations grounded in reality (or as close to it as you can get).

- To create successful feedback experiences when performance needs to improve: 1) invite employees to walk you through their own self-assessment, 2) ask them if they are looking for feedback, and 3) ask them to clarify the specific kind of feedback they are seeking. Next, decide whether and how to respond: 1) check to see if the feedback you are considering offering fits their request, and 2) provide your feedback as objectively, factually and non-judgmentally as possible.

- Honest, positive feedback is one of the greatest accelerants for improvements in your employees' performance. Offer positive feedback often, either recognizing past accomplishments or acknowledging a demonstration of their character.

- Strive to achieve a ratio of 4:1 or 5:1 in terms of balancing positive interactions and feedback with negative interactions and feedback.

- To help employees reap the benefits of feedback, walk them through setting improvement goals that have a good chance of being achieved.

- Share what you notice using four-dimensional listening by offering "feedback on the spot." This will help employees feel heard and may help to surface important topics.

- Even if the ideas in this chapter seem strange and different to you, at least try them out in small doses and give them a chance.

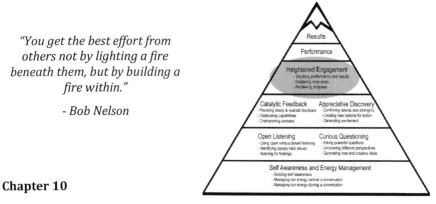

"You get the best effort from others not by lighting a fire beneath them, but by building a fire within."

- Bob Nelson

Chapter 10

Skill #6: Heightened Engagement

We talk about Heightened Engagement both as an outcome of using the other skills on the Coaching Conversations Trailmap, and also as the skill of building on Heightened Engagement – translating engagement into action, high performance and results.

During each of your coaching conversations – as you question with curiosity, listen openly, discover appreciatively and offer Catalytic Feedback – you are creating Heightened Engagement. At times, you will see the visible result on their face. Your employees will increasingly feel heard and valued for their contributions. As a result, they will be encouraged to use their strengths more often and feel more motivated. They will become more trusting of you and feel more confident about sharing ideas and proposing solutions to emerging issues. They will start to take more initiative when it comes to problem solving. These are some of the practical outcomes of Heightened Engagement.

Now the question is: what can you, as a manager-coach, do to translate that engagement into productive, targeted action that generates organizational results? We've identified three key areas you can focus on:

- ***Targeting performance and results*** by ensuring alignment with organizational goals

- ***Designing next steps*** by clarifying actions to be taken, building commitment and anticipating potential obstacles

- **Reviewing progress** by debriefing after the employee follows through, to identify transferable learning and celebrate achievements.

The rest of the chapter is dedicated to walking through each of these areas in more detail.

One analogy that is sometimes used to describe this process of moving toward clarity, focus and closure is that of "landing the plane." Rather than "talking things to death" or leaving things "up in the air," there comes a time to steer the conversation and nail down tangible decisions and commitments, leaving your employee with a sense of forward momentum and the expectation of success.

Targeting Performance and Results

This aspect of building on Heightened Engagement is about ensuring alignment with organizational goals, and clearly establishing what success will look like (i.e., what will constitute high performance and good /excellent results). Achieving this can be as simple as starting with questions such as:

- Let's summarize: what are you ultimately trying to accomplish with this? Which of the organization's goals does that help us make progress on?
- How does this fit with your existing priorities? With the team's priorities?

This is really just a test or check on alignment with organizational goals and priorities, which may already have been implicit in your conversation.

This is also the time to address standards and expectations around performance and results for this task/project. As a manager, you could simply lay out the parameters; as a manager-coach, you may want to consider getting their input first and thinking it through together:

- What will success look like on this task/project – how will we know if you've done a good job?

- What size do you envision the finished product to be?

- What are the essential elements that need to be contained in the solution? What issues and considerations must the solution address?

- How much latitude were you hoping for in crafting the approach to this solution? How much input would you like from me?

- Who else needs to be consulted on this before you have the whole picture?

If, as you listen to their responses, there is something missing or you hear something that won't work for you as the one ultimately accountable for the end result, then you will need to communicate that clearly at this point. Let them know where they truly can take the lead in shaping their work, and where you need to have input. If you think of this as part of the plan-implement-evaluate cycle of a project, then this is about coaching them through the planning phase.

Finally, if you've already been having conversations with that employee about particular areas of their performance that they are working towards improving, you could ask: *"You've talked about improving your ability to _____; how could you use this opportunity to do that?"*

Designing Next Steps

This is the stage where you can walk an employee through: clarifying what action steps they will take, anticipating potential obstacles, building their commitment to follow through, and agreeing on how progress will be tracked and reviewed. Table 12 summarizes the kinds of questions you might want to ask to cover each base.

Table 12: Questions for Designing Next Steps

Focus	Questions
Identifying and clarifying action steps	What are you responsible for in this? What does the deliverable look like to you? How clear are you on the scope of this? Who else do we need to include in this project? What's the first step you need to take to get started? What else will you need to do? By when? What additional information, support and resources do you need?
Anticipating potential obstacles	What might get in your way? How could you handle that? Or, what are some options for dealing with that if it comes up? What support do you need from me around problem solving?
Building commitment to follow through	On a scale of 1 to 10 (1 being "not very" and 10 being "very"), how committed are you to following through right now – honestly? If the answer is 7 or below, ask: What would bring that up a notch? What are you looking forward to seeing at the end of this?
Agreeing on how progress will be reported	When and how will you update me on your progress? Who else needs to be kept informed? At what stage in the project do you imagine you might want to check in with me most often?

Some conversations may not be as action-oriented as the questions in the table suggest; however, they can still yield increased insight, understanding or learning as their outcome. The insight might be as simple as clarity about an adjustment they want to make in their own mindset, attitude or perspective; or it might be a better understanding of some additional context, factors or issues they need to take into consideration in a future decision. In those cases, simply asking *"What are you taking away from this conversation today?"* can be a good way to check in and see what conclusions they have come to. An action item may even flow out of those conclusions.

Reviewing Progress

At this stage, you'll want to initiate a short session with your employee to debrief after they have followed through – either with some of their next steps, or with the entire effort (depending on the scope of what they're working on). Your role as a manager-coach then is twofold: first, to help identify transferable learning, and second, to celebrate achievements. Here are the kinds of questions you could ask:

- "What's better now than it was before? How did you contribute to that?"

- "Where have you made progress?"

- "What else did you accomplish? How do you feel about what you've accomplished?"

- "What did you learn in the *process? How can you apply that learning to something else you're working on right now?"*

- "What needs to happen next to make sure we don't lose ground on this (to maintain progress)?"

- "What needs to be celebrated? What would you like to celebrate in all this?"

This is also a great time to offer them any genuine praise or recognition, if it's warranted based on their performance.

You may also want to take the opportunity to assess how the trust in your relationship with this employee has been influenced by your recent work together by asking questions like:

- "How well did we communicate in this project/process?"

- "Are there areas where I could be doing a better job of supporting you in my role?"

- "Were there any points in this project/process where you feel I broke any agreements or understandings that we had with each other?"

As we noted in Chapter 2, trust is a key ingredient in the coaching relationship and needs to be monitored and maintained over time.

Beginning Another Cycle With a Stronger Foundation

You'll notice the kinds of questions we're asking at the end of this stage bring a sense of completion; that's because Heightened Engagement is the pinnacle of the Coaching Conversations Trailmap. It acts as a bridge to the performance and results that you, your coachee, and your organization are all looking for. It also sets you up for greater success during the next cycle because you've deepened your relationship and built trust with that employee. You'll now be starting your next trek up the Trailmap from a stronger foundation.

What to Take Away from This Chapter

- Heightened Engagement is both an outcome of using the other skills on the Coaching Conversations Trailmap and also the skill of building on that Heightened Engagement – translating engagement into action, high performance and results.

- We use the analogy of "landing the plane"; rather than leaving things "up in the air," there comes a time to steer the conversation toward nailing down tangible decisions and commitments.

- The first element of translating engagement into action is to ensure the employee's course of action supports and aligns with an organizational goal, and to clearly establish what success will look like (what will constitute high performance and excellent results).

- Next you can walk an employee through: clarifying what action steps they will take, anticipating potential obstacles, building their commitment to follow through, and agreeing on how progress will be reported.

- After the employee has followed through – either with some of their next steps or with the entire effort – your role is to help identify transferable learning and to celebrate their achievements.

PART III: PRACTICAL TOOLS FOR HAVING COACHING CONVERSATIONS

"Before everything else, getting ready is the secret to success."

- Henry Ford

Chapter 11

Setting the Stage for Successful Coaching: Preparing Yourself and Your Employees

By this stage in the book, we hope you are feeling excited and motivated to try out the coaching skills outlined in Part II. Before diving in haphazardly, there are a few things we suggest you do to set the stage for successful coaching:

- Give yourself permission to have fun

- Give yourself room to learn

- .Introduce your employees to coaching and let them know what to expect.

This chapter is devoted to these topics. In the following chapter, we'll talk about how to prepare for an upcoming coaching conversation (Chapter 12). Then in Chapter 13, we'll provide you with some sample outlines (sequences of questions) to guide you through some of the most common coaching conversations.

Give yourself permission to have fun

We bring our philosophy about relationships in the workplace to our coaching and leadership style. Some people successfully integrate fun and humour into their leadership; we believe it's possible to do the same with coaching as well. In one case, we coached a senior leader toward bringing more fun to work, not only for his benefit but also for that of the people who worked for him and with him. It makes a huge difference to employee morale and helps create a positive work environment.

We invite you to see coaching as something that can be fun – for you as the manager-coach and for the employee. The issues you work on with your employees are certainly important, but for the most part, they are not life and death (with some exceptions, depending on your profession and business). We encourage you to find the joy or humour in a given situation – it's okay to laugh and have fun during a coaching conversation. At the very least, you can always bring fun in at the closing of a conversation to end on a positive note: *"Just before we finish up, what could you do to have fun with this?"*

Give yourself room to learn

Everybody struggles when they start coaching; please find a way to remind yourself that it's okay to try although it may not be perfect. In our experience, employees are looking for you to come alongside them as a coach (rather than simply direct them) and will cut you a lot of slack when they see you making an effort. As an example, even though Curious Questioning is about asking simple questions, it can feel awkward at first. Claire Simpkins, one of our fellow Associates at Tekara, offers this encouragement:

> *As you learn to become more coach-like, don't worry if you ask the right questions ... relax. Be curious, stay in that place of inquiry, and be present. Trust your own instincts about what you need to ask. At first, new coaches worry: 'What if the questions I ask don't create a deep, transformational moment for the other person?' Just ask the questions and then be there to listen and you'll go a long way.*[37]

In other words, it's not the perfect question that makes the difference – it's the invitation your curiosity offers them.

We encourage you to start small and build from there. As a busy manager, it would be easy to set overly ambitious goals and then get frustrated, discouraged and give up altogether. Instead, set some targeted, realistic goals. In Part IV of the book, we provide you with a guide to a four-step development process to gradually incorporate more and more coaching into your daily interactions with employees, at a pace that's manageable for you.

Introduce Your Employees to Coaching and Let Them Know What to Expect

Now that you've got greater awareness about the value of coaching and a new set of skills, it's easy to assume your employees and colleagues are ready and eager for you to coach them. Some managers dive right into coaching employees only to have people looking at them with a "deer caught in the headlights" expression. *"Huh? Where is this person coming from?"* Those of slightly more cynical nature will chalk up your new approach and behaviours to a new management fad that will soon pass.

Shifts in your approach to management may be welcomed by people in the appropriate moment, but, they can often leave people wondering *why* you are making such a shift. Is this just the temporary influence of some training – or are you really opening up a safe space to have coaching conversations? Unless people sense your intentions as a coach are authentic, it can be difficult to build a safe environment for those conversations to occur. This comes back to our discussion of trust in Chapter 2. It takes time to establish the foundation of trust which allows for successful coaching. Fortunately, there are a few things you can do to help accelerate the process:

1. **Demonstrate genuine care for your employee as a person.** This involves getting to know a bit about their life and interests beyond work (if you haven't already). Follow-up on what they shared with you in previous conversations and ask how things are going.

2. **Communicate simply and clearly about what coaching is and how you plan to use it.** Before having your first coaching conversation with a particular employee, we suggest you have a brief conversation with them first to introduce the notion of coaching and your motivation for using it.

Since a picture is worth a thousand words, one way to explain coaching is to draw a quick sketch of Figure 2 ("Roles During a Coaching Conversation") from Chapter 1, showing how the "coachee" focuses on the issue on the table while the "coach" focuses on the coachee's thinking process. You can contrast this with past conversations where you might have been focusing on the issue on the table as well (by giving advice, suggesting solutions, or taking over and solving the problem for them).

Think about other key messages you want to communicate that will help to address key sources of mistrust. *Why are you wanting to try out coaching? What can they expect from you?* Anticipate some of the questions that might come up for them or "buttons" it might push. For example: *Are you only planning on coaching them, or other members of the team as well (i.e., are they being singled out somehow)? Is this somehow "remedial?" How does coaching fit into the annual performance management cycle?*

3. ***Be transparent about the fact that you are now wearing two hats.*** You can clarify you will still wear your manager hat which keeps you focused on business results and what's best for the organization. At the same time, you'll be adding a coach hat which will help you focus on their learning, growth, development and success. You'll also want to clarify how coaching fits into the performance management process. Wearing your manager hat, you'll still be setting performance goals and expectations. Wearing your coaching hat, you'll be helping them grow and develop to meet those expectations. This will involve taking advantage of learning opportunities as they occur, in real-time.

4. ***Give them some choice in the matter.*** Part of our human nature is to resist change – especially if we feel we don't have a choice. One way to help employees warm up to coaching in light of that very natural tendency is to give them some choice. Let them know that from now on, when they come to see you, you'll be giving them a menu to choose from. *Would they like you to: a) just listen, b) coach them, or c) give them input/advice? Or maybe coach them first – and then give them advice if needed? Also, which part of the situation would they like to be coached on?* You'll be surprised at how introducing the element of choice can increase their receptivity to coaching.

5. ***Involve them in your learning process.*** Be open about the fact that coaching is an area of learning and growth for you. Let them know that as you practice your new coaching skills, you'll be asking for their

feedback to help you improve. For example, at the end of each coaching conversation, you can ask some very simple questions like: *"How was that coaching for you?"* and *"How can we make the coaching more effective next time?"* Act on their feedback to the best of your ability. By doing this, you are role modeling the process of learning on the job, with the support of colleagues (which is what you'll be offering them the chance to do as you coach them). As it turns out, by making yourself vulnerable as a learner, you also increase the chance of developing a stronger connection with that employee. Research shows that how much we reveal about ourselves helps us "click" with other people, because vulnerability invites a reciprocal response.[38]

By taking the time up front to prepare both yourself and your employees for the coaching experience, you're laying the foundation for success.

What to Take Away from This Chapter

- When you start practicing your new coaching skills, give yourself permission to have fun with it, and give yourself room to learn at a manageable pace. .

- Prepare your employees for the experience of being coached, meet with each of your employees briefly one-on-one to: explain what coaching is, describe how you plan to use it, outline what they can expect from you now that you are wearing two hats (manager hat and coaching hat), give them the choice of deciding when they are open to having coaching conversations, and invite their feedback to help you improve.

"The best conversations are the ones prepared ahead of time ...
Many potentially fruitful conversations go nowhere, because they are like ships
without rudders. They wander aimlessly or go in circles.
If the facilitator is the helmsman, the intent of the conversation is the rudder. A
good conversation needs both a good facilitator and a focused intent."

- Brian Stanfield

Chapter 12

Preparing for a Coaching Conversation

We strongly encourage you to start experimenting with Curious Questioning and Open Listening whenever the opportunity presents itself. You don't need a special occasion – start today. Ask one curious question during your next conversation and then listen openly to the response.

At the same time, there are some conversations that require a bit more planning, especially if you want to use a coaching style from start to finish. Although a particular outcome can't be guaranteed, preparation goes a long way toward creating a conversation that has a good chance of advancing an agenda (yours and theirs), creating shared learning and strengthening the relationship in the process. Preparation also leaves you feeling more equipped and confident about practicing your new skills.

In this chapter, we'll cover – and review – a number of topics related to preparing for a specific, upcoming coaching conversation:

- Factors to consider when choosing the timing and setting for the conversation

- Managing the duration/length of a coaching conversation

- Cultivating the four coaching mindsets

- Using the "Ask-Tell" conversation planning tool.

- Using the skills of self-awareness and energy management to prepare yourself before the conversation

Choosing the Timing and Setting of a Coaching Conversation

We encourage you to be mindful of the time of day when scheduling a conversation. For many of us, we hit a lull in our physical energy around 2 to 3 pm – it's part of the circadian rhythm or wake/sleep cycle we experience every 24 hours. Whenever your daily low point is, avoid that time slot for coaching conversations if at all possible. If you do need to have it then, recognize that you may need to spend a few minutes beforehand to boost your energy by moving or doing some active breathing.

As for the setting, it's up to you and your coachee to agree on what works. Here are a few options and factors to consider. If you would like to set a different tone for your coaching conversations, you can do this in a couple of ways. The first is finding a setting outside your own office – perhaps an internal meeting room. This can help to free you both from distractions (as will turning off your cell phones, pagers and blackberries). The second way to create a departure from the norm is altering the seating arrangements. By habit, we will take a seat directly across from another person. Unfortunately, this can set up a slightly adversarial dynamic – the feeling of a face-off with one person in the hot seat – even when that's not our intent. If instead, we sit beside them, it sends them a different message: we're in the same boat, facing the same direction, looking at the same thing, facing the challenge together. Admittedly, this message seems subtle, but it will register at some level. If nothing else, it signals a change.

Choosing a more informal setting (for example, outside the office, in a park or in a restaurant) could either free up the conversation, or send a cue that this is "off-duty" or social time, suggesting a lack of focus. In large part, it depends on your ability to comfortably initiate and steer the conversation in that setting where there may be more visual distraction and noise. If this kind of setting works for you (and the other person), you might even consider having your coaching conversation while walking together, in order to keep your physical energy high throughout the interaction. This also has an advantage similar to that of sitting side-by-side at a table, as you have less direct eye contact while you walk. Since direct eye contact can feel intimidating at times (especially if we've just been asked a powerful question and need time to reflect), walking alongside may actually free up the other person to think more clearly and creatively.

For spontaneous or spur-of-the-moment coaching conversations, it may be tempting to just stay in the hallway (or wherever the conversation starts). However, finding a more private space will allow you the flexibility to follow the conversation wherever it needs to go in the event that it takes an unexpected turn; for example, if the employee discloses something personal or vulnerable, or if the conversation turns to a discussion of an interpersonal issue.

Managing the Duration or Length of a Coaching Conversation

Most coaching conversations take 20 to 45 minutes. Some will take as few as 5 or 10 minutes; others, an hour or more. It will depend on many factors: the topic or issue, the person, the context. Do your best to assess and allocate the full amount of time you think will be needed. In some cases, you may find yourself winding up the conversation only to peel another layer off the onion (or move to another funnel, as we describe below). In that case, you may need to schedule another time to pick up the conversation again.

Here's how we visualize the flow or shape of most coaching conversations. Sometimes you get approached by someone who has clarified in their own mind exactly what problem, opportunity or decision they are grappling with, exactly where they are stuck, and what they want from you out of the conversation. More often though, they haven't reached that point in their thinking yet. So imagine that you are starting the conversation at the mouth or top of a funnel. Your role as the coach is to help move the conversation down through the funnel, helping them get clear about what they want out of the conversation.

Once they've clarified their focus – the specific problem or opportunity they want to look at with you – then the conversation changes shape again. As you begin to explore options and generate possibilities, you're back to the top of a new funnel, brimming with ideas. Again, your role as the coach is to help move the conversation down through the funnel, helping them get clear, this time, on how they want to move forward. Over the course of a coaching conversation, you'll likely move through a series of funnels.

If you don't have time to make it through the next funnel, then simply agree on a time to come back to the conversation later.

Adopting the Four Coaching Mindsets

This section is a simple reminder to review the four mindset shifts (Table 13) that can make the difference between an effective coaching conversation and a typical workplace conversation.

Table 13: Four Mindset Shifts of Effective Coaches

	From	To
Mindset Shift #1	Treating colleagues as lacking and inadequate	Treating colleagues as creative, resourceful and capable
Mindset Shift #2	Assuming that you already know	Listening for what your colleagues know
Mindset Shift #3	Telling people what to do	Asking people how they want to contribute
Mindset Shift #4	Trying to understand the underlying causes of a problem	Finding a solution to the problem

One helpful habit to build is to do a quick assessment of your mindset as you head into a coaching conversation:

- What mindsets are you walking in with ("From" column)?

- Which one mindset shift do you most need to focus on during this conversation?

- How could you equip yourself to stick with the shift through the conversation? For example, could you jot something on your notepad to remind yourself?

- What questions could you prepare and jot down ahead of time to help you stay in that more positive mindset?

This last question is something we address using the "Ask-Tell" coaching conversation planning tool, which we'll introduce next in this chapter.

Using the "Ask-Tell" Coaching Conversation Planning Tool

It's relatively easy to imagine using a coaching approach when someone approaches you for advice or guidance. We're not as used to imagining how to keep our coaching hat on even in situations where we are the ones initiating the conversation – and bring our own agenda as managers. The key is to move as much as possible from telling, to asking, by leading with questions just as you would in any coaching conversation.

The "Ask-Tell" planning tool (Exercise 5) is a very simple tool you can use to help you plan for this type of conversation. Take a sheet of paper and draw a line down the middle. Label the left-hand side "Tell" and the right hand side "Ask." In the left hand column, jot down notes about what you would like to tell the other person during the conversation – all the information, decisions and messages you would like to convey. In the right hand column, jot down the questions you would like to ask them – all the perspectives, information and input you are hoping to gather.

Exercise 5: Ask-Tell Conversation Planning Tool

TELL: What do I want to tell them?	ASK: What do I want to ask them?

Initially, you may find that it's much easier to fill out the "Tell" column. That is understandable; it's what you've been trained to do. But see if you can then challenge yourself to fill out the "Ask" column as well. Think back to the coaching mindsets we described in Chapter 4 and reviewed in the previous section in this chapter. Assume or imagine the person you're going to be speaking to has information and a perspective which will help build or improve on your thinking about the situation so far. Assume they know something that you don't know – and you need to know. Now your challenge is to figure out how to call forth their relevant knowledge and ideas. Look at each item on your "Tell" list and ask yourself:

- What additional information or different perspective might they have on that?

- What assumptions might I be making that need testing?

- What could I ask them that would invite them to become part of the solution?

Here is an example (see Table 14). Imagine you are trying to get an employee to look at how effectively they are completing their tasks. You've witnessed firsthand some instances where they haven't hit the mark, and at the same time, you believe they could improve.

Table 14: Sample of a Completed Ask-Tell Exercise

TELL: What do I want to tell them?	ASK: What do I want to ask them?
You're not hitting the mark in the areas that you are responsible for.	How well do you think you're doing right now? What are you most proud of with respect to your work? What requires the most improvement? On a scale of 1-10 (1 is poor, 10 is excellent), how well do you think you're performing on the job? What feedback are you getting from me either verbally or non-verbally (i.e., how do you think that I think you're doing)? What's working? What's not working? If we could make one change, what would it be?
You seem more dependent on instruction than I had hoped.	If you could make one request of me right now, what would it be? What would you need in order to feel more comfortable taking more initiative on this moving forward? What are you hoping to hear from me that you haven't heard yet?
We need to meet more regularly to review progress.	How often do you think we need to meet right now for this project?

As you finalize your outline for the conversation, ask yourself: What percentage of the time in a conversation do you normally spend talking versus listening with this person? What do you want to do this time? Remember that even a small shift in the direction of asking/listening is likely to have a positive impact on the quality and outcome of the conversation.

The "Ask-Tell" tool is especially helpful if you're planning to have a conversation that feels emotionally charged in any way for you. That was exactly the situation that one of our clients, Gail, faced in her working relationship with a contractor whom she was responsible for supervising, and whose performance she was finding disappointing. Applying the "Ask-Tell" tool to her situation, Gail discovered it was possible to have an emotionally charged conversation in a different and much less volatile way. Having thought through the "Ask" and "Tell" columns made it easier both to navigate the conversation and to hear what the contractor had to say.

As it turned out, the contractor was already aware of not meeting expectations and felt upset about it. The contractor had some frustrations of their own about the lack of clarity around the scope of certain parts of the project. As a result of having gone through the "Ask-Tell" planning exercise – and leading with curious questions instead of with judgements about the contractor's performance – Gail and the contractor were able to identify what was working and what was not, and to agree on some changes to address both their concerns. Most importantly, they did so without the conversation spiralling into an unproductive cycle of defensiveness and blame. In fact, the contractor almost perceptibly sighed with relief about being able to talk about what was happening.

The other advantage for Gail, when she listened first, was a change in perspective. She realized that she did not have all the relevant information about the factors affecting the contractor's performance. If she had barged ahead by sharing her own disappointment and judgements based on incomplete information, she might have needlessly placed blame and started an emotional chain reaction.

The further payoff of investing time up-front to do "Ask-Tell" planning is an increased level of trust and candour heading into future conversation. You'll also likely increase the probability that the other person will feel comfortable coming to you sooner when there is an issue down the road.

One note of clarification is needed here. We are not suggesting you "Ask" when you have made a final decision about something and simply need to communicate it. There is nothing more frustrating for an employee or colleague than being invited to provide input only to find out later that your mind was already made up. We're suggesting using the "Ask-Tell" exercise in situations where you:

- are uncertain about having reliable, complete information

- need cooperation, support and engagement from others in order to move forward successfully

- need improved performance from others in order to move forward successfully.

Managing Your Energy Heading Into the Conversation

The ideal state to be in when you head into a coaching conversation is: physically energized, emotionally connected to yourself and the other person, mentally focused, and 'spiritually' aligned with what matters most. Of course, we can't always achieve that ideal state on demand, but there are simple and practical things we can do to prepare physically, emotionally, mentally and 'spiritually' for a successful coaching conversation. Table 15 summarizes our best tips.

Table 15: Practical Tips for Managing Your Energy Before Heading Into a Coaching Conversation

Physical	***Make sure you've eaten in the last 2 to 3 hours – if not, grab a bite.*** If you haven't had anything to eat in the last 2 to 3 hours, your body is already going into survival mode, and is beginning to shut down certain mental functions. Emotionally it's triggering chemical reactions that are going to make it much more difficult to be engaged in the conversation.
	Get up and move. Have you gotten up and moved in the last 90 minutes – or have you been sitting in your chair for an extended period of time? When it comes to fueling our brains to function well during a coaching conversation, we need both glucose (sugar) and oxygen. Food gives us the glucose; movement gets oxygen circulating. If you want to be at your best, take a walk around the building, climb a flight of stairs, raise your heart rate for a few minutes, or go outside and take some deep breaths. This is especially important if the conversation will take place in the middle of the afternoon when most of us experience a lull in our physical energy.

Emotional	***Clear the emotional decks.*** Take a moment to do a quick scan of your emotional energy. If you're feeling relaxed, optimistic, and hopeful, then you're in an ideal state to coach. If on the other hand you're feeling more tense, anxious, frustrated, worried, or overwhelmed, then the challenge is not to carry that into your conversation. How do you shift your emotional state? Here are a couple of things you could do in as few as 2-3 minutes that can have a big impact: • close your eyes and think of something that brings you joy (e.g., fun times, the face of a loved one, a hilarious situation that made you laugh, a place you enjoyed visiting, etc.) • briefly listen to some music you enjoy • close your eyes and picture a point in the not-to-distant future when you'll have some relief from the emotions that are weighing on you (e.g., how much fun you'll have when the weekend comes; how good you'll feel when you finally have that talk with your boss; how good you'll feel when the speech you're so worried about is finally over; how good you'll feel when the day is done and you're finally snuggled down in bed ready to sleep) We often underestimate how effective these small acts can be in shifting our emotional energy.
Mental	***Minimize interruptions.*** Make sure that you will not be interrupted during your coaching session. Turn off your computer screen and the volume on your computer speakers, turn off your cell phone unless you are specifically "on-call." ***Park the distractions.*** In your mind's eye, picture taking anything that is vying for your attention and put it in a drawer. Close this imaginary drawer knowing that you can take everything out again after your coaching session. ***Picture yourself coaching successfully.*** See yourself coaching as if you were watching a movie of yourself from the audience (rather than imagining yourself looking out from the eyes of the actor/actress). In as much detail as possible, picture how you will move, how you will stand/sit and hold your shoulders and upper body, how and where your eyes will be focused, what you will sound like, what your facial expression will be like. The more detail you add and notice, the more likely you will embody all that during your actual coaching session.
Spiritual	***Get clear on what you hope to accomplish in the conversation.*** Take a moment to reflect. What would make this coaching conversation a success? What are you hoping to learn? What are you hoping to practice? What impact are you hoping it will have on your relationship with the person you're coaching?

In the next chapter, we offer you a series of conversation guides or maps – sample sequences of questions you could use to walk through conversations on some of the most common topics of coaching conversation.

What to Take Away from This Chapter

- Be mindful of the time of day when scheduling a coaching conversation. If possible, avoid mid-afternoon time slots since this is a daily low point for physical energy.

- When choosing a setting for the coaching conversation, consider ways to set the tone you want (formal/informal), liberate the conversation, and minimize distractions. Explore alternatives to your office: another meeting room or something outside the office altogether. Consider either sitting or walking side-by-side to signal that you're having a different kind of conversation.

- Allocate sufficient time for a coaching conversation (30-45 minutes) and be prepared to schedule a follow-up session if you run out of time.

- Remind yourself of the coaching mindsets before heading into a conversation: treat your colleagues as creative, resourceful, and capable; listen to what your colleagues know; ask people how they want to contribute; focus on finding a solution.

- Use the "Ask-Tell" planning tool to map out how you will use curious questions to guide the conversation. This tool is especially useful if you are heading into an emotionally-charged conversation.

- Although we can't always achieve the ideal internal state for coaching on demand, there are simple and practical things we can do to mobilize our physical, emotional, mental and 'spiritual' energy for the conversation.

"If I had an hour to solve a problem and my life depended on the solution, I would spend the first 55 minutes determining the proper question to ask, for once I know the proper question; I could solve the problem in less than five minutes."

- Albert Einstein

Chapter 13

Guides for Having Coaching Conversations on Specific Topics

Conversations can solve a problem, generate commitment, bond a team, generate new options, build a vision, shift working patterns, build relationships, create focus and energy, and cement resolve – it all depends on the topic of conversation and the way you and the other person navigate your way through it. In this chapter, we provide you with sample roadmaps for walking through some of the most common themes of coaching conversations. Here are the recurring scenarios we address:

1. Coaching an employee to solve a technical problem

2. Coaching an employee through addressing an interpersonal issue (i.e., helping them prepare for a difficult conversation they need to have)

3. Coaching an employee for improved performance

4. Coaching an employee for heightened engagement and motivation

5. Using coaching skills to improve your interactions and relationship with your own boss

In each case, we provide examples of the kinds of curious questions you can use in sequence to guide the conversation. Pick and choose which questions may be helpful to your situation versus asking them all. Our intention is not to be prescriptive – these roadmaps are examples only. Think of these guides as a starting point, or springboard, for your own preparation and planning for a coaching conversation.

Scenario 1: Coaching an Employee to Solve a Technical Problem

Helping an employee come up with their own solution to a technical problem is often one of the first types of coaching conversations that managers choose to practice. In Table 16, we offer you a variety of questions you could ask in this scenario; you will likely only need a few at each stage of the conversation.

Table 16: Guide to Helping an Employee Solve a Technical Problem

Coaching Goal at Each Stage of Conversation	Sample Questions to Ask Your Employee
Clarifying the Issue (and what help they want from you)	• What's up? What's happening? What's going on? • How can I help you? This last question is very useful to ask. It helps the person clarify what they want from you: they may want permission to execute a solution they've already thought through; they may be seeking advice or a sounding board; they may just want to inform you. If they just want permission or to inform you, just follow through and wrap up the conversation. But if they are looking for advice, keep going. • What's most concerning/important for you in all this? • Help me understand your concern more fully … • What makes it so important that this be handled properly? • What's the bottom line? • What's the real challenge (problem or opportunity) here?
Envisioning Possible Ways Forward	• What do you think would work best here? • What have you already thought of trying? • What's worked well for you in the past in a similar situation? How could you adapt that creatively to this situation? • What if the problem went away overnight – what would be happening in the morning that would let you know?

	• When does that solution (or "problem-free" situation) happen sometimes already? How could you build on that and make it happen more often? • I've seen you do this successfully before (*use this only if it applies*). What worked then? • If you were advising a colleague about how to handle this, what would you suggest? • What would someone else (e.g., a competitor) do?
Confirming Next Steps	• Of all the ideas you've come up with, which one(s) do you want to try? • What additional information do you need? • Whose input or support do you need to move forward? • What do you need from me as you move forward? • What will you do next? By when? • Is that a realistic timetable? • If you need to wait (e.g., for additional information) before moving forward, what else can you do to stay productive in the meantime? • Are there any potential obstacles you need to address to make sure you're able to follow through on time?
Generating Excitement & Building Commitment	• What excites you most about the approach you've chosen? • What will be easiest about this for you? • What's the best part of this for you? • On a scale of 1 to 10, how committed do you feel about following through? *If they answer 7 or below:* What would bring that up a notch?
Agreeing on How Progress Will Be Reported	• When and how will you update me on your progress? • Who else needs to be kept informed? • When do you imagine you might want to check in with me again?
Bringing Closure	• Did you get what you needed? • What are you taking away from this conversation?

	• What was most helpful about this conversation for you?
Gathering Feedback to Support Your Development as a Coach	• How was that coaching for you? • How can we make the coaching more effective next time?

Scenario 2: Coaching an Employee Who Needs to Have a Difficult Conversation

Over time, employees will likely approach you with problems that are either technical or interpersonal in nature. Either way, it may be that resolving those problems requires the employee to have a difficult or emotionally-charged conversation. Your biggest gift to them as a coach can be to help them walk into the conversation prepared – and equipped – to have it as constructively as possible.

Linda Sartorio, a senior manager in a utility company, describes a situation where she applied her coaching conversation skills to help an employee:

> I was working with a management trainee who found herself to be in an unrealistic situation in a large headquarters where she was actually asked to take on two full-time jobs without a lot of support. She was becoming really frustrated and emotional so I had a direct coaching conversation with her and basically asked her about how she thought that she could solve the problem and what she needed to talk to her superiors about. We walked through what she wanted to say in the conversation where she was really able to focus on what she needed, and what her expectations were to solve the frustration for her. At the end of the day, she took the next step and had a conversation with her superiors where they were able to work out a realistic solution. That turned out really well, and she's in a much better place. [39]

In Table 17 we've outlined the kinds of questions you could use to help an employee prepare for a difficult upcoming conversation. You'll notice we have incorporated the "Ask-Tell" conversation planning tool we introduced in the last chapter.

Table 17: Guide to Coaching an Employee Who Is Preparing for a Difficult Conversation

Goal at Each Stage	Sample Questions to Ask Your Employee
Clarifying the Issue	• What's up? What's happening? What's going on? What's wrong? • What's most concerning/important for you in all this? • Help me understand your concern more fully … • What makes it so important that this be handled properly?
Clarifying your role as coach	• How can I help you? • It sounds like you might need to have a tough conversation with so-and-so to resolve this – would you like some help preparing for that? • Would it be helpful if we talked about how you might handle the situation/conversation?

Exploring stakes and desired outcomes	• What's really at stake for you here?
	• What do you hope to accomplish by having this conversation?
	• What's the specific outcome you would like to create as a result of this conversation? For example, would you like to:
	   o Feel heard and understood?
	   o Request changes in the other person's behaviour?
	   o Create a shift in your own behaviour?
	   o Make agreements about how to handle a situation?
	   o Renegotiate/clarify expectations of each other?
	• What would be the best possible outcome from your perspective?

Mapping the Conversation using the	• What could you say at the beginning to set a positive tone?

"Ask-Tell" Tool	This is a great place to introduce the "Ask-Tell" conversation planning tool.
	
	 • What do you want to "tell" the other person? What do you really want the other person to know about:
	     o How you see what happened (or is happening)?
	     o How it's affecting you?
	     o What you'd like to see happen next time or in the future?
	 • What do you want to "ask" the other person?
	     o How do they see what happened (or is happening)?
	     o How is it affecting them?
	     o What do they want to see happen next time or in the future?
	
	 As a coach, you may want to encourage them to use the "Ask-Tell" approach in their conversation: either by starting the conversation with "asking" or by "telling" just enough at the beginning and then alternating between asking and telling.

Exploring how to manage emotions during the conversation	• How might you be triggered in discussing this topic? What might help you to stay focused and constructive during the conversation? • How might the other person get triggered in discussion on this topic? What can you do to make this less likely?
Confirming Next Steps	• What will you do next? By when? • What do you need from me as you move forward? • Is there anything that would stop you from having this conversation? How could you handle that?
Generating Excitement & Building Commitment	• What's your biggest hope for this conversation? • How are you feeling about the approach? • What will be easiest about this for you? • If you imagine this all being resolved, how do you feel? • On a scale of 1 to 10, how prepared do you feel to have the conversation? If 7 or below: What would bring that up a notch?
Agree on Follow-Up	• Will you let me know how it goes?
Closing Questions	• Did you get what you needed? • What was most helpful about this conversation for you?
Gathering Feedback to	• How was that coaching for you?

Support Dev.	• How can we make the coaching more effective next time?

Scenario 3: Coaching an employee for improved performance

In this scenario, we review the suggested approach that we outlined in Chapter 9 on Catalytic Feedback. Whether your employee approaches you for feedback about their performance – or you choose to initiate a conversation to seize a "teachable moment" using a coaching style – we recommend following the same steps (Table 18) to help them learn from experience.

Table 18: Guide to Coaching an Employee to Learn from Experience and Improve Performance

Goal at Each Stage	What You Might Say or Questions You Might Ask
Have them assess their own performance	• How are you feeling about the situation and your role in it? • How did the _____ go (e.g., meeting with client, presentation to committee, etc.)? How do you think you did? How do you think it went? • How are you feeling about it in this moment? • If they're focusing exclusively on what went wrong and what they didn't do well, prompt them with: Talk me through what went well (or what's going well) … And what else? • On a scale of 1-10, how pleased are you with your performance? What would a "10" look like? • What did you wish you'd done differently (more of/less of) in that situation? • What else did you learn from the experience?
IF NEEDED - Build their confidence in their ability to improve	Sometimes, an employee will get overly negative and stuck in their thinking at this stage, believing that they are unable to improve. They've developed a story or self-image they have of themselves as "always" doing something wrong (e.g., "I always lose my nerve/confidence around so-and-so") or "never" getting something right (e.g., "I never remember details like that"). Listen for the words "always" and "never" in their speech.

	If this crops up, your role is to remind them that they are capable – not by heaping on praise, but by helping them hunt for exceptions and times when that problem doesn't happen (or only partially). For example, you could ask:[40] • Is that true – that you really never/always _____? • Can you think of a time when you did/didn't _____? What was different about that time? • When is the problem not so bad? If you think of the most recent time the problem didn't happen, what transpired instead? • What do you suppose you did to contribute to that difference? How did you do that?
OPTIONAL – Provide your own feedback	It's entirely possible that by this point in the conversation, your employee will have already demonstrated they are fully aware of any shortcomings that affected their performance. If so, there's no need to reinforce it through your own negative feedback. Instead, your job as coach is to help them shift their focus to what they can do differently next time. If, however, your employee does not seem to be aware of having performed poorly, then offering some feedback may be helpful. First, <u>gauge their receptivity</u> by asking: • Are you looking for feedback? Would feedback be helpful? Next, <u>get them to set the parameters</u> of the feedback they are interested in and willing to receive: • What would you like feedback about specifically? • What kind of feedback would be helpful right now? • So, just to clarify, you'd like to get better at _____ (e.g., delivering presentations, behaving appropriately with senior leaders, etc.). What kind of feedback would you like from me to help with that? • Are you asking me for feedback on how I see you ____? Offer your feedback in the form of non-judgmental observations that are as factual and objective as possible. • You can use the following phrasing: "I notice that when you _____ (observable behaviour without judgmental labels attached), I (or other people) react/respond by _____." • For example: "I noticed when you sped up and started talking more quickly near the end of your presentation,

	people began to get restless and looked like they had stopped listening."
Plan for improved performance moving forward	• What could you do differently to prevent that from happening again? • What would success look like for you if you did it well next time? • What could you do differently based on what you learned this time? • You've talked about wanting to improving your ability to _____; how could you use _____ (upcoming event/opportunity) to do that? • What are you planning to do next time? • So when it comes to improving your ability to _____, what would success look like for you three months from now? What steps could you take to work towards that? • So it sounds like you've got an action plan to: 1)_____, 2)_____, and 3)_____. Does that sound right? • Is there anything I can do to support you with that? • Would you like to get together before your next _____ (meeting, presentation, etc.) to see how things are going as you prepare for that?
Building commitment to follow through	• What's going to be the best part about doing better at this? • On a scale of 1 to 10 (1 being "not very" and 10 being "very"), how committed are you to following through? *If the answer is 7 or below, ask:* What would bring that up a notch?
Gathering Feedback to Support Your Development	• How was that coaching for you? • How can we make the coaching more effective next time?

Scenario 4: Coaching an Employee Who Appears Less Engaged and Motivated

Sanjay Dutt, CEO of RvaluE Learning describes employee engagement, and the role of the manager-coach in building and maintaining it this way:

[Engaged employees] willingly and enthusiastically work towards the organization's goals and want to succeed...the role of coaching is to help them grow and achieve success in whatever they're doing...If you want high performance, you need people who are committed and capable. The goal of your coaching is to get the capable people to succeed, and as a result, get them committed to what they're doing. [41]

So what do you do if you notice that an employee seems less enthusiastic, motivated, and committed, and engaged? Mark Frezell at WestJet tells the following story about a coaching conversation he had with a crew member who seemed disengaged, especially by WestJet standards (where there is an overall culture of high engagement):

[I was on a flight] and I went to the back to talk to the crew; it's sort of an old habit. On this particular crew, one member was pretty disengaged for WestJet. [He was making comments like] 'I just do my job,' 'I don't give anyone feedback,' 'I don't try to correct anyone else's performance or behaviour,' and 'I keep my head down and stay under the radar.' What ended up happening was a good coaching conversation around his situation and how he got to that place... [I asked] a lot of questions... We kind of went back in history around some of the previous things that had happened with a [particular] in-flight [work experience] that had shaped his perception. Then I was calling the truth out. I remember specifically saying: 'I believe that you're disengaged.' We talked about: 'What does that mean for the business?' I told him that my goal is: 'I want to re-engage you in the business.' So there was a bit of telling [but mostly] asking...In the course of the conversation – it was probably about fifteen minutes – there was a moment in time where his perception changed and the lights came on. You could see it in his face when he realized: 'Oh, you know what I'm doing? I'm doing this to myself. I'm disengaged: how do I turn that

around?' It wasn't me telling him. It was a conversation that he participated in to change his perspective. [42]

Table 19 outlines a possible approach to initiating and having this type of conversation with an employee who seems less engaged than they used to be (or could be). Just to clarify, in this scenario, we imagine an employee who is still performing well (or well enough) at a technical level. It's more their level of enthusiasm, motivation, interest and commitment that seems to be flagging. This might show up as some combination of withdrawal, irritability, low energy and a decreased investment in creating successful outcomes. At a more intuitive level, you might perceive the person's internal spark or flame is burning low, or that they are "stuck" in some way.

Table 19: Guide to Coaching an Employee About Their Level of Engagement

Goal at Each Stage of the Coaching Conversation	Things You Might Say and Questions You Might Ask
Initiate the Conversation, Clarify Your Intent and Provide Context	Start by opening with a short statement that sets the tone and communications concern as opposed to judgment or criticism. • Thanks for making the time to talk. I just wanted to check in with you – not about your performance, but about how you're doing. Provide some non-judgmental feedback that lets them know what you're observing in their behaviour. For example: • I noticed when we had our last project/team meeting, you seemed kind of withdrawn, not participating in the conversation as fully as you normally do. • Or, lately I've been noticing … Then let them know how you're interpreting their behaviour. • I find myself thinking that maybe you're feeling less enthused, less interested, and less motivated these days. • I find myself making up a story that … Clarify your intent in bringing this up with them • It worries/concerns me when I see you

	• because it's important to me that you feel motivated and engaged, not only because it affects how you are at work, but also for your own sake. • If there's any truth to what I'm thinking, I wanted you to know that I want to do whatever I can to help.
Test Your Assumptions	• I'm curious – is there any truth to what I've just said? • Is any of that true for you? ...
Gain a Better Understanding of the Employee's Perspective	• What can you tell me about what's been happening for you? • What's happening from your point of view? • How are you feeling about your work lately? • What's working and what's not working for you these days in your role? • What's shifted? • What's changed? • What do you think is missing for you right now? • How long has this been going on for you? • I know sometimes it's tough to figure these things out. If you had to guess, what do you think it might be? • When is the last time you remember enjoying your work? What were you doing? What was interesting/motivating for you about that? If you compare that to your current situation, what's missing? NOTE: As uncomfortable as it may be, you also need to leave room for the possibility that part of your employee's disengagement relates to their relationship with you as their manager. To explore this possibility, you can start by asking: • What role am I playing in how you're feeling? Watch their body language closely as they respond. If you sense a high level of discomfort or avoidance, then the employee may not feel safe enough with you to be honest on this topic. In that case, you can say and ask: • What's important for me is your engagement. I want to work with you and do whatever it takes to see that grow back. Is there someone else you could talk to either here at work, or outside work, that might be able to help you get some perspective on this?

	• Who else might be a good person for you to talk with this about?

Listen closely and openly and use curious questions to let them know you're really interested in understanding what's happening for them. You may get a whole range of responses to your questions. Here are just a few of the things you might hear (either stated directly or inferred):

- I'm struggling with something outside of work, in my personal life.
- I just don't feel like what I'm doing really makes a difference or has much of an impact.
- I had a really bad experience with someone here at work and I've been pretty shut down since then.
- I don't feel challenged by my work anymore.
- I'm not learning anything new these days.
- I don't really get to work on the kinds of things that really interest me.
- In my role, I'm not really using my strengths or doing what I enjoy most. Or, if I was given the chance, I think I could do a really good job of _____, but I never get to do that.
- I just have too much on my plate, and I never know where to start (unclear priorities).
- I'm having a hard time with one of my colleagues.
- Ever since _____ happened (e.g., we changed systems, we downsized, etc.), it just hasn't been the same (or things have gotten worse, harder to deal with).
- There are just so many things in the way of completing or achieving anything meaningful around here (i.e., barriers to productivity, "red tape," etc.).
- I never get to do anything creative/collaborative.
- I don't really get much say about my work – everything is decided for me, from how I spend my time, to who I work with, to how I do the work. I just wish there was a little more flexibility and latitude for me to use my own judgment and creativity.
- I'm not sure I'm really suited for this job (or that this job is suited to me).

| OPTION A - Exploring Possibilities to Increase Their Engagement in Their Current Role/Situation | Your questions at this stage will depend largely on what your employee has just shared with you about what's happening for them. Here are a few generic questions you might consider using:

• What do you need to get back to feeling more motivated and engaged?
• What would it take for you to feel more motivated and engaged?
• What kind of support do you need? From whom?
• How can I support you?
• What do you need from your colleagues to make this |

	work?
OPTION B – Exploring Possibilities to Change Their Role/Situation	• What would it take for you to feel more motivated and engaged? • What change in scene/job/responsibilities might do it for you? • How do you feel about considering making a shift like that?
Designing Next Steps	• Out of all the options we've talked about, what's going to work best for you? • So we talked about the possibility of _____, _____, and _____. What would you like to explore further?
Agreeing on Follow-Up	• What would you like to do about this? • When do you want to talk about this next? • When should we meet to talk about this again? • I hope it's okay if I keep sharing with you what I'm noticing as you move forward on this.
Closing Questions	• What was most helpful about this conversation for you?

Scenario 5: Improving your interactions with your own boss

One often overlooked application for coaching conversation skills is in interactions with your own boss. Although you are clearly not coaching them for development, there are creative ways you can apply Curious Questioning, Open Listening, Appreciative Discovery and Catalytic Feedback when talking with your direct supervisor. We explore a few here.

Using Curious Questions

Curious Questioning can be a very valuable skill to practice with your boss. For example, you may be noticing that your boss seems more distracted and impatient than usual, seeming overwhelmed. You may even be getting frustrated as it's becoming more difficult to gain their undivided attention when you need it. Rather than leading with your frustration, you could choose curiosity instead and ask questions like: "What can I do to help you with whatever is most pressing for you right now?" or "What can I do to help make your job easier and speed your plans along?" Once they sense your intent to be supportive, they are far more likely to be open to hearing about your needs as well.

Another great application for Curious Questioning is whenever we're feeling very anxious to please. In those situations, we can easily tell ourselves that the fewer questions we ask – and the sooner we get out of our boss' hair – the better. On the other hand, if we don't ask enough questions, we won't get the information we need to actually please, in order to deliver the desired results. Here are some sample questions you might ask to get clarity when a task or project is being delegated to you:

- "What would success look like for you in this project?

- "From your perspective, what is the key deliverable?"

- "What do you envision the finished product to be?"

- "What are the essential elements you want to see contained in the solution?"

- "How much latitude do I have in crafting the approach to this solution?"

- "What won't work for you?"

- "What, if anything, could get in my way that I should know about?"

- "Who else needs to be consulted about this before I have the whole picture?"

- "How – and how often – do you want to be updated on progress?"

- "At what stage would you like to have further input?"

While you may know your boss' style and preferences well, you may also be pleasantly surprised to uncover valuable information and perspectives by getting more curious with your questioning.

Offering Appreciation

In one of our recent Coaching for Engagement™ training programs, we tried a little experiment. This was an in-house program being delivered to a group of participants within a single organization, some of whom were there with their bosses. When we got to the section on appreciation and positive feedback, we put out a bowl of candies and told the group that at any time, they could approach anyone in the room and give them one of the candies; the only rule was they also had to express appreciation for something that person had done or some aspect of their character. Guess who got the fewest candies? The bosses in the room. We talked with the group about that trend, and got curious about what lay behind it. Most people said they were reluctant to give their boss any praise – even when they genuinely had some to offer – because they didn't want to be perceived as "sucking up" or "brown-nosing."

Our bosses are not less hungry for appreciation than any of us. Clearly, you don't want to go overboard – and you do want to keep any positive feedback grounded in the truth. Apart from that, our encouragement is to make it a point to appreciate your boss too – not just your employees and your colleagues.

Asking for Feedback: Why Not Invite "Feed-forward" Instead?

As we explored in the chapter on Catalytic Feedback, we are all hungry for feedback because we have an underlying drive to improve our performance. The only problem with feedback is it focuses on the past, and tells us what we did wrong back then, without addressing what we could do differently and better moving forward. That's where "feed-forward" comes in.[43] Feed-forward focuses on the future, offering practical suggestions for improvement or change; so rather than asking your boss for feedback, why not invite feed-forward instead?

Here's how you could do that:

- Pick one particular skill you would like to improve or behaviour you would really like to change.

- Describe the skill or behaviour briefly and simply (e.g., "I want to be more decisive" or "I want to develop my strategic thinking skills").

- Ask your boss to give feed-forward in the form of two suggestions for the future to help you achieve a positive change in the skill or behaviour you're targeting. *Specifically ask that they refrain from giving ANY feedback about the past – only ideas for the future.*

- Listen openly and closely to their suggestions and take notes without commenting on their suggestions – not even to say *"That's a good idea."*

- In closing, thank them for their suggestions.

Who knows? Your boss may even follow your example and ask you for feed-forward as well.

What's Next

Now that you have the four coaching mindset shifts, the six core coaching skills, and the practical advice and tools from these last three chapters, all under your belt, it's time to turn our attention to bridging the gap between learning/knowing and doing. In Part IV of the book, we'll help you develop a personal action plan that will help you gradually introduce coaching into your daily routine and conversations, until it becomes a natural part of your management style.

PART IV: TAKING ACTION: BRIDGING THE GAP FROM KNOWING TO DOING

"Who you are speaks so loudly that it drowns out what you are saying"

- Ralph Waldo Emerson

Chapter 14

Bridging the Knowing-Doing Gap: The Process of Becoming a Manager-Coach

At this point in the book, you may find yourself thinking the coaching skills and tools we've covered are very basic; there's some truth to that, since it's all grounded in common sense. You may also be feeling a flush of excitement about the possibilities that open up for you when you start applying the skills. But as with many aspects of managing, the *biggest challenge is not knowing the mechanics of the skills, but actually using them.* When we get back into our work environment – especially in situations where the stakes are higher – we can easily slip into our default patterns of communication with employees despite our best intentions. While the skills are easy to understand, trying them out in your workplace conversations may initially feel uncomfortable, awkward or tiring.

In this chapter, we want to:

- reassure you that it is normal and to be expected

- guide you through a simple put powerful four-step process that will leave you with a personal action plan for gradually incorporating more and more coaching interactions into your day

- encourage you to stick with it.

If you're clear you would like to adopt a coaching style of management, then investing the time in working through this chapter will help you cross the "knowing-doing" gap, while you begin to reap the rewards of coaching almost immediately.

The Stages of Learning[44]

Managers don't become masterful coaches overnight – they get there one conversation at a time. As your experience grows, you'll gradually move through four key stages of learning (see Table 20). The good news is you've already moved through the first one just by reading this book!

Table 20: Stages of Learning

Learning Stage	Key Phrase	Description
Unconscious Incompetence	"I don't know that I don't know how to do this."	I'm not aware of what coaching is, or how it could help me improve my communication to build greater employee engagement.
Conscious Incompetence	"I know that I don't know how to do this, yet."	I've become aware of the skills and mindset shifts needed to coach for engagement. I'm starting to practice these new skills, and sometimes feel disappointed or frustrated with the results or with the pace of my progress.
Conscious Competence	"I know how to do this, and can do it increasingly well, as long as I pay attention."	I continue to use and build my coaching muscles, and still remind myself what to do and how to do it. I'm seeing improvement, and feeling more confident, although I am still sometimes uncomfortable or self-conscious during a coaching conversation.
Unconscious Competence	"I know how to do this and I do it well without even having to think about it."	I'm performing well as a coach, and it's become part of my approach to working with people. I no longer have to think about "putting on my coaching hat" when necessary – I just do it without thinking about it whenever it's appropriate. Coaching feels natural to me.

The hardest stage to be in is the second one: Conscious Incompetence. It's in this stage that you run the risk of getting bogged down in your own self-judgment as you try something new. You might even feel stuck on the diving board, deciding on the "right" place for you to dive in. There is no right place to start – other than starting small and building from there. Rather than creating a huge to-do list of things to remember when coaching, focusing on just a few simple but high leverage activities will build your momentum. Moving from Conscious Incompetence to Conscious Competence will take time and energy; along the way, having a plan will help keep you focused. That's why we strongly encourage you to follow the development process we outline in the rest of the chapter. It is designed to help you create a personal plan that includes realistic development goals. It's also a place in the book you can return to if and when you get discouraged, and need to figure out how to get back on track.

Following the Four-Stage Development Process[45]

Your development journey is going to be unique, based on your particular strengths, values, skills and experience. In our experience, though, there are four common steps successful managers follow along the way:

1. **Get clear on your purpose.** This step is about tapping into your motivation to learn and grow into a manager-coach. Start by asking yourself: *Why are you making this change in management style? How will you measure your success?*

2. **Assess your starting point.** The next step is examining how you currently coach (or don't) and identifying both your strengths and biggest opportunities for development.

3. **Create your plan.** This involves mapping out a 30-day learning path, specifying the coaching habits you'll focus on, and outlining the support mechanisms you'll draw on to keep moving forward.

4. **Implement, measure, and review.** Over the 30-day period, you'll follow through on your plan, tracking your progress as you go, and reviewing it both weekly and at the end of the 30 days. You do this to make sure you notice what works, what doesn't, and what else you're learning along the way. Your observations will help you decide how to shape your next 30 days.

The rest of this chapter is dedicated to walking through each step in more detail, and providing you with practical tools along the way. In Step 2, we'll give you a link to our online assessment tool; in Step 3, we'll give you a template for your plan and show you a sample; in Step 4, we'll introduce you to a Learning Log you can use to track your progress towards your goal.

Step 1: Get Clear On Your Purpose

Although it may seem self-evident, knowing and articulating why you are doing this is a critical first step. You may buy into the idea of coaching, having been convinced of the benefits it could provide both for you as manager and for the people you lead. But without a clear connection between coaching, and the impact that you uniquely want to have as a manager, your efforts will soon become nothing more than a series of New Year's resolutions. What's going to motivate you to try out coaching skills – even if it feels uncomfortable at first? What's the long-term gain for you as a manager that will motivate you to start and get over any initial hurdles?

In other words, what is the "win" in coaching for you? Here are some questions to consider:

- If you were looking ahead six months from now, what would a successful outcome look like for you (as it relates to developing and using your coaching skills)?

- How will coaching enable you to live out one or more of your core values more fully?

- What would you like the people you lead to say about you specifically six months from now?

- How will coaching for engagement enable you to achieve your team's and your organization's strategic objectives for this year?

There aren't any right or wrong answers here. Taking the time to reflect on why you are about to embark on this journey – and what you hope to accomplish along the way – is an investment which will payoff during the inevitable periods where you're tempted to stick with your existing communication patterns.

Although it isn't vital to come up with a sentence that encapsulates how you define success from this learning process, many people do find it helpful to create a statement. Here are a couple of examples:

- "Success for me will be...having at least one coaching conversation every day and as a result, <u>seeing an improvement in my employee's ability to solve problems</u>."

- "Success for me will be...consciously using my coaching skills in at least 5 interactions every week, and as a result, <u>seeing my employees taking more initiative</u>."

What is your statement and definition of success?

_____

_____

_____

Step 2: Assess Your Starting Point – How Are You Doing Now?

It's been said that, as human beings, we all have an infinite capacity for self-deception. Consequently, it can be challenging to accurately assess how well we currently coach. However, it's still worth giving yourself a chance to be objective about it; self-assessing your existing skill level can be a helpful starting place when deciding where to focus your development initially.

We've created a simple assessment tool to help you evaluate your current coaching skills. You can complete the assessment online at: *www.coachingforengagement.com* or use the one provided in Appendix A. If you complete the assessment online, your results will be scored automatically, and you'll receive a customized report, as well as information on how to access the other resources and tools related to this book.

As you complete each question, go with your gut reaction. Don't over think it. Your initial response is usually the most accurate. This is not a contest. No one else needs to see your scores; they are simply a snapshot of your starting point.

Please complete your assessment before continuing.

Reviewing Your Results

Earlier in this book, we discussed Catalytic Feedback; assessments can be one form of it. It's natural to focus on our weaknesses when reviewing assessment results, perhaps even to beat ourselves up a little about why we scored low in a certain area. In our experience, it is actually more helpful for new coaches to focus primarily on practicing and building their skills using areas of strength. There will always be time to chip away at weaknesses later; taking a strengths-based approach initially allows you to get over some of the emotional "humps" during the Conscious Incompetence stage of learning that we talked about near the beginning of this chapter.

Here are a few questions you can ask yourself as you review your results, to make sure that you pay enough attention to your strengths as well as areas for development.

- What are the bright spots (3 to 5 highest scores) in your results?

- What do your strengths tell you about yourself?

- What surprised you about the results?

- What elements of your leadership style are reflected in your results?

- What were the weaknesses (3 to 5 lowest scores) in your results?

- How could I begin to leverage my strengths more in my next coaching conversation?

- How can I use these strengths to coach *myself* when I'm struggling as a coach?

In preparation for the next step in the process (creating a development plan) let's look at the areas where you could see some quick gains:

- Which coaching skills do you feel the most motivated to practice?

- Which coaching skills do you feel comfortable with already, but haven't been using as consistently as a manager?

- Which coaching skills do you think will be the easiest to begin using right away?

This will give you some options to choose from in the next step, when we'll invite you to narrow your list and pick a single area of focus.

Step 3: Create Your 30-Day Development Plan

Many of the clients we've worked with have found it helpful to narrow the scope of their coaching skills development plan to just one month. Why a 30-day plan? Why not 90-days or an annual goal? We've found leaders who focus on one specific change at a time, and pour all their energy into that 30-day period, are far more likely to create sustainable results and shifts in their behaviour. Learning a new skill will require you to make changes and move outside your comfort zone, all of which takes energy. It's best to take small bites, and focus on behaviours you have control over, rather than on specific outcomes you don't. A 30-day goal is usually just large enough to be significant to your long-term development, but not so big you will run out of willpower and discipline before achieving it. In other words, you won't be tempted to put it off for a few months until the due date gets closer – you'll need to get started right away! If you start and don't completely succeed, you can always adjust your plan and start again.

Coaching for Engagement

Here are the basic ingredients of an effective 30-day plan:

- **A clear learning goal.** This is the one thing, if accomplished in the next 30 days, that will have the most impact on your development as a coach on the engagement of your team.

- **A set of 'performance rituals'.** Think of a ritual as a 'habit in the making'. It's a simple, small, specific action or behaviour which moves you toward your goal – that you commit to practicing intensely over the 30 days. The idea is that if you do these things consistently, they will start to become habitual for you, requiring less and less conscious effort on your part. Eventually, you'll start doing them automatically. Think of a ritual as a tool for accelerating one very specific part of your coaching skill set through the learning stages – from conscious incompetence, right through to unconscious competence – so that it becomes a new positive habit.

- **A support system.** No one becomes a great coach without the support of others. Who do you need to enroll in your learning plan to support you on your journey? Who could encourage you to stick with it? A colleague? A mentor? A friend outside work? If you have the benefit of your own internal or external coach, you may want to discuss how they can support you as well.

In the pages that follow, we're going to spend some time delving into the art of designing helpful performance rituals, and then wrap up our discussion by showing you a sample 30-Day Development Plan.

Creating Performance Rituals for Coaching

The concept of performance rituals has been used for decades in the arena of high performance athletics, and is now making its way into the development of leaders in other high performance arenas such as business, healthcare, and government. When top athletes are improving their performance, they focus their development on making very small changes. As they master each small change, then they are able to execute very complex physical routines – and

178

maintain mental toughness – even under extreme pressure. In other words, they no longer have to rely on willpower, discipline and conscious thought to perform at their best.

It turns out this way of learning and training makes a lot of sense given how scarce willpower and discipline are for all of us. Dr. Jim Loehr and Tony Schwartz, authors of *"The Power of Full Engagement"* explain: *"A growing body of research suggests that as little as 5% of our behaviours are consciously self-directed. We are creatures of habit and as much as 95% of what we do occurs automatically or in reaction to a demand or anxiety."*[46] This means whenever we're trying to practice a new skill, we're tapping into a scarce resource – a very small percentage of our attention and energy that is available for making moment-to-moment conscious choices to act in a different way. We want to make sure we use that scarce resource wisely, and turn our new skills into habit as quickly as possible.

That's where performance rituals come in, helping us to accelerate the process of making a new habit a natural part of our behaviour (see Sidebar 4).

Sidebar 3: How Top Athletes Train and What Coaching Managers Can Learn From Them

When learning to swim the front crawl stroke, proper technique is critical. Swimming faster is rarely about the athlete producing more force to propel them through the water. Instead, the biggest gains are made from learning how to streamline or reduce the resistance an athlete's body has in the water.

Becoming streamlined begins with good head position and balance. It's natural for swimmers to lift their head when they come up for air, but the corresponding effect is their legs drop, resulting in more drag. They move slower. To correct this, the athlete needs to focus on dropping their chin to their chest.

So for a few weeks, the athlete will focus on a very simple performance ritual: "concentrate on tucking your chin to your chest," or "keep your neck straight when you rotate to breathe."

For those few weeks, they stay focused on that one small piece of technique. There may very well be other things they need to work on as well: stopping their legs from dropping too low, rotating more fully on each stroke, pushing their hips down, and making sure their hand enters the water closer to the 2 o'clock position. But tackling all of them at once would be way too much to focus on. And perhaps more importantly, some of these elements are things they do not have control over - they are the effects of body misalignment in their upper body. So instead, they focus on just one small factor that they have control over – lowering their head position.

This requires a great deal of mental energy on the athlete's part initially because it doesn't feel natural at first. But by focusing on this simple performance ritual, within a few training sessions, it soon begins to feel normal. Within a few months it becomes a habit. No longer does it require any mental focus or energy. Now they can focus that energy on a new performance ritual.

Slowly, performance rituals like this one add up to dozens of habits which propel their high performance. The Olympians we see reach the podium at the Olympics are the product of hundreds, if not thousands of little performance rituals developed over years, one step at a time.

So it is with masterful coaching.

Let's take something simple to start with – how you breathe when you're coaching. As strange as this may sound, when stressed, we tend to take shorter, shallow breaths. This reduces our capacity for engaging fully in the moment. It reduces the amount of oxygen our brain has access to, and makes it easier to slip into survival mode (discussed in Chapter 5). To counteract this, one of the first things you can do is remind yourself to just breathe! The ritual would be taking a deep breath (inhaling for 5 seconds). To help yourself remember, picture a stop sign with the word "Breathe" on it. Then when you're in a situation where you feel uncomfortable, anxious, angry, or tense (e.g., someone has just said something provocative), imagine that stop sign with the word "Breathe." Then, just do it – take a moment to take a deep breath before speaking or doing anything else. This 5-second pause can be enough to regain your composure, or reset yourself to ensure you are focused on the opportunity in the conversation again. Practicing this simple performance ritual in conversations will require a great deal of energy initially, but eventually it will become a habit. You'll no longer have to think about it.

Here's another example. If your learning goal is Open Listening, and your performance ritual is to avoid interrupting (shut up and listen!), then you might use the W.A.I.T. (**W**hy **A**m **I** **T**alking) acronym to help you remember. You may find it helpful to actually write WAIT out on the top of your notepad when going into a meeting so you'll see it periodically, but eventually you won't need to rely on any visual cues.

Here are four keys for designing your own rituals:

1. **Focus on doing something new versus stopping an old behavior.**
   For example, rather than trying to stop yourself from jumping into advising and solution mode, focus on being more curious and focused on the individual's thought process versus the solution itself.

2. **Be specific about the timing (when) and behavior (what).**
   General rituals such as "be more curious" have no teeth. It needs to be clear how to accomplish specific behaviours; for example, at the beginning of each conversation (*when*) I will ask myself, *"Who do I need to show up as in this conversation – coach or director (what)?"*

3. **Only focus on one to three rituals at a time.** Creating a laundry list of things you want to work on right away will usually result in overload, followed rapidly by disillusionment. To take advantage of

willpower as a scarce resource, focus on no more than one to three rituals at a time. As soon as the new ritual becomes a habit, you can add a new one to your list, so you are only working on a small number at a time.

4. **Be prepared to invest a lot of energy on a ritual initially.** It's easy to underestimate how difficult it can be to make seemingly simple changes. Our existing patterns of thinking and relating to other people are deeply engrained. Even if you stumble a bit at first, commit to sticking with it for at least 20 to 30 days and you should see progress.

Table 21 summarizes the key elements of a simple but effective 30-Day Development Plan, and also provides a sample.

Table 21: Summary and Sample 30-Day Development Plan

Plan Element	Description	Tips	Example
Learning goal	The one thing – if accomplished in the next 30 days – that would have the most impact on your development as a coach, and on the engagement of your team.	Keep your goal simple and realistic.	To get better at Open Listening.
Performance rituals and cues	A simple, small, specific action or behaviour that moves you toward your goal – and that you commit to practicing intensely over the 30 days.	Focus on doing something new (versus stopping an old behavior). What will you do from now on (instead of what you used to)? Be specific about the behaviour and timing – precisely what you will do and when you will do it.	Ritual - When I feel the urge to interrupt, I will re-focus on listening to understand what the other person is saying. Cue – I will write the W.A.I.T. (Why Am I Talking) acronym at the top of my notepad.

| Support system | People who are willing to provide support in the form of listening and encouragement to follow through. | Remember that we all need support when we're learning something new. Knowing that you'll be talking to someone else about your progress can help you stay motivated (it's like putting positive peer pressure on yourself). | Before I get started, I will ask my colleague Jim/Sue if I can do a quick weekly 10-minute "check-in" with them to help me stay on track. I'll ask them to just listen and encourage me to stick with it. During my check-ins, I'll tell them: - what's working well - what's not working well - what I'm noticing/learning along the way. |

Step 4: Implement, Measure and Review

High performance athletes are known for their attention to detail and rigorous tracking of their progress. One of the most basic tools is a daily training log to keep track of each important element they are working on.

We've created a basic tracking sheet for your performance rituals and performance cues (ways you remind yourself to perform your ritual in the moment). You can download it from the resource section of our book website: *www.coachingforengagement.com*

Either at the start or conclusion of each day, take a minute to reflect on how well you implemented your performance ritual in conversations (on a scale of 1 to 5). Don't beat yourself up about a day when things fell short – just focus on the next opportunity. At the end of each week it can be helpful to see if there are any patterns developing. Which rituals are easier to implement than others? Were there any benefits you didn't intend on receiving when you first designed the ritual? Are there days of the week when you seem more effective than others? Why do you think this is the case?

Everyone experiences setbacks in their progress. It's not a matter of if – but when – you'll hit some barriers, whether it's the internal culture of your organization, a difficult employee, or your own internal critic. Recognizing up front that some coaching conversations will be better than others, and setting realistic expectations will help with this.

Staying focused on what you are trying to accomplish does not require judging or punishing yourself when you fall short. But setbacks can provide useful input worth evaluating. We can learn as much from our failures as we can from celebrating and reinforcing our successes.

Bottom line: be curious, make any small adjustments if necessary, and don't jump to any conclusions until the end of your 30-day experience when you can look at your results as a whole.

Review and Repeat

At the conclusion of your first 30-day period, take a few minutes to celebrate what you have accomplished, wherever you improved, even if you didn't reach your intended goal. Before you even start implementing your plan, make sure you've marked the end of the 30-day period on your calendar to remind yourself to do this. You may want to include someone from your Support System in the celebration.

If you find yourself falling short repeatedly with a particular skill or performance ritual, several explanations might be possible:

It may be the goal you set is simply too ambitious to accomplish in 30 days and needs to be implemented in smaller progressive steps.

- It may be the performance ritual isn't ideal for what you are trying to accomplish and needs to be restructured. Or the cue you've designed isn't helping you remember what to do in the moment.

- In some cases, there may be a benefit or payoff to sticking with your existing behaviour. This causes unconscious resistance that is powerful enough to keep you from moving forward. For example: *"When I offer my employees advice instead of helping them find their own solution* (existing behaviour), *I feel useful and valuable in my role* (payoff)." To make progress, you'll need to work at shifting those beliefs.

After reviewing your 30-day progress, you're ready to start a new cycle again, selecting a new goal, and creating a plan to support you. This becomes a life-long cycle of development towards coaching mastery.

You Can Do It: Overcoming the Fear of Getting Started

One manager we worked with shared her experience of getting started:

> *I recall the first time I got the opportunity to coach one of the senior managers in my organization. I was nervous, feeling like a bit of an imposter, wondering how long it would take before the leader realized I was way out of my league. I took a deep breath and focused on the one thing I knew I had control over in that moment – how intently I listened. I reminded myself that I wasn't there to rescue them. As the executive began explaining their situation I was amazed by how focused I became. The chatter in my own mind subsided and I simply focused on making sure I understood how the situation the individual was describing was affecting them. I simply listened and gave him space to talk.*
>
> *As the conversation progressed for about 10 minutes I could hear the initial stress and tension in their voice dissipate. I hadn't spoken more than two or three times. Suddenly, in the process of just verbalizing his thoughts on the situation he was concerned about, an insight occurred to him. It didn't come from me. And as we wrapped up the conversation a few moments later he commented, 'Wow, you're really good at*

this. Thanks for that, it really helped me to get your perspective on this.' But I hadn't shared my perspective at all!

All I did was listen and articulate the thoughts he had expressed back to him. It was the first time I really realized the power of coaching, and how just focusing on one simple change, my listening, I could begin to see results immediately.[47]

What to Take Away from This Chapter

- Clearly define how you and your team will benefit when you adopt a coaching style as a manager.

- Assess both your strengths and challenges as a coach, use your strengths to help create momentum quickly, and create support for your weaknesses.

- Building new skills is best achieved through the skilful design and use of performance rituals and cues.

- Surround yourself with support and chart your progress. Set backs are inevitable, but small adjustments can reap huge dividends.

*"Some dismiss the 'soft stuff' of communication
because it seemingly does not relate directly to results ...
[but conversations] are the best, most reliable tool available
for influencing others and gaining the buy-in and committed action
needed to achieve real business objectives."*

- Phil Harkins

Conclusion

At the beginning of the book, we set out to share with you two key insights, and equip you with some helpful tools:

- Insight #1 - Coaching is not simply a technique for dealing with performance issues. It is a powerful business practice that can increase results by increasing engagement.

- Insight #2 - Coaching is first and foremost a mindset, not just a set of tools and techniques. When we adopt a coaching mindset, we take a far more positive and appreciative view of others, and that translates into a different way of treating them.

- Tool Set #1 - A set of simple and practical tools, including six core coaching skills and a variety of tools to help you plan and conduct effective coaching conversations.

- Tool Set #2 - A simple action plan outlining how you'll start using coaching conversation skills and tools in your everyday interactions and build your confidence along the way.

Most of all, we wanted to persuade you that coaching is a very worthwhile skill to acquire as a manager. The need for better people skills to heighten employee engagement is growing, and will keep on growing. We also wanted to make it easy for you to start down the path of learning and practice. There is no one right way to coach, so our intent was simply to provide you with a trail map you could use to orient yourself to the new territory, and to find your own way to make coaching work for you.

With awareness comes the opportunity to choose something better. We hope that armed with your increased awareness of the advantages, benefits and power of coaching, you'll choose to find a way to make coaching a part of your management style and daily interactions.

Ripple Effect: From Coaching Conversations to a Coaching Culture

As for the future of coaching conversations in the workplace, we believe there is reason to be optimistic that the trend is catching on – and will continue to grow. As coaches ourselves, we've witnessed firsthand the powerful impact of coaching conversations on individual development and engagement. As facilitators of the Coaching for Engagement™ program, we've seen what a dramatic difference it makes when the managers we train start using the skills and tools in this book. Organizations and their people need the engagement that coaching conversations can help build, and we believe managers are more than capable of stepping up to the challenge.

You might be encouraged to hear that in some organizations, coaching conversations started in pockets, then rippled steadily out, reaching a critical mass. In those workplaces, efforts are now underway to nurture a "coaching culture," making coaching conversations the norm ... but that's the subject of another book. The important thing is: it can all start with you, one coaching conversation at a time.

To continue your journey, explore the additional resources, and engage with other leaders and managers committed to engaging their team at:
www.coachingforengagement.com

APPENDIX A: Coaching Skills Self-Assessment

Instructions:

Please read through the descriptions for each coaching skill and rate yourself from 1 (never) to 5 (always) according to how frequently you currently use the coaching skill or behaviours. Keep in mind that this is just a subjective assessment. Your initial gut reaction to each question is usually the most accurate.

Once you've completed the assessment, calculate your scores for each section and your overall score.

A brief interpretive guide on your score is provided following the assessment, with book page references to further information on each skill or area of focus.

An online version of this assessment is also available at:

www.coachingforengagement.com

RATING SCALE:

5 = Always : I never miss an opportunity to do this where appropriate

4 = Often : I frequently do this as appropriate, few missed opportunities

3 = Sometimes : I do this about 50% of the times, miss about 50% of the opportunities

2 = Seldom : I infrequently do this, many missed opportunities

1 = Never : I very rarely or do not do this at all

1. Self-Awareness and Energy Management	Score (1 - 5)
a) Building self-awareness – noticing the energy you bring into a coaching conversation and how it fluctuates during the conversation	
b) Managing your energy <u>before</u> a conversation – preparing physically, emotionally and mentally - clarifying your purpose and intention for the conversation	
c) Managing your energy <u>during</u> a conversation – maintaining a positive physical, emotional and mental state - reminding yourself about your intention for the conversation	
SECTION TOTAL:	

2. Curious Questioning	Score (1 - 5)
a) Asking powerful questions – seeking to understand what others assume, value and want to accomplish	
b) Uncovering different perspectives – being genuinely curious about what others think	
c) Generating new and creative ideas – sparking the kind of innovative thinking that produces new ways of seeing things and new possibilities	
SECTION TOTAL:	

RATING SCALE:

5 = Always : I never miss an opportunity to do this where appropriate

4 = Often : I frequently do this as appropriate, few missed opportunities

3 = Sometimes : I do this about 50% of the times, miss about 50% of the opportunities

2 = Seldom : I infrequently do this, many missed opportunities

1 = Never : I very rarely or do not do this at all

3. Open Listening	Score (1 - 5)
a) **Using open vs. closed listening** – remaining respectful of what others are really saying and want to contribute, not just listening for what you want to hear or have them do	
b) **Identifying deeply held values** – listening for the values and aspirations that motivate others most powerfully	
c) **Listening for feelings** – respecting the deeper agenda for the things that matter most to others	
SECTION TOTAL:	

4. Appreciative Discovery	Score (1 - 5)
a) **Confirming talents and strengths** – looking for the unique capacities and genius of others, so you can build together on their best	
b) **Creating new options for action** – exploring the opportunities to channel talents and strengths in service of the organization's goals	
c) **Generating excitement about positive possibilities** – connecting with a strong source of motivation	
SECTION TOTAL:	

RATING SCALE:

5 = Always : I never miss an opportunity to do this where appropriate

4 = Often : I frequently do this as appropriate, few missed opportunities

3 = Sometimes : I do this about 50% of the times, miss about 50% of the opportunities

2 = Seldom : I infrequently do this, many missed opportunities

1 = Never : I very rarely or do not do this at all

5. Catalytic Feedback	Score (1 - 5)
a) **Providing timely and realistic feedback** – being real about what will help achieve success and what will get in the way	
b) **Championing successes** – setting small, highly leverage goals that have a good chance of being achieved	
c) **Celebrating capabilities** – catching someone doing something right and reinforcing it with praise to provide the incentive for further improvement	
SECTION TOTAL:	

6. Heightened Engagement	Score (1 - 5)
a) **Targeting performance and results** – ensuring alignment with organizational goals	
b) **Designing next steps** – clarifying actions to be taken, anticipating potential obstacles, building commitment and agreeing on how progress will be reviewed	
c) **Reviewing progress** – identifying transferable learning and celebrating achievements	
SECTION TOTAL:	

OVERALL TOTAL:

BRIEF INTERPRETIVE GUIDE

Skill	Areas of Focus
Self- Awareness & Energy Management p.59 - 68	• **Building self-awareness** • **Managing our energy before a conversation** • **Managing our energy during a conversation**
If your score = 6 or below	Self-Awareness and Energy Management are a foundational aspect of having great conversations. Your energy management rituals are not supporting you or the conversations that you want to be having. Refer to pages 59 – 68 in the book for ideas to help build your four kinds of energy.
If your score = 7 to 11	Self-Awareness and Energy Management are a foundational aspect of having great conversations. You are doing some things well, and probably understand the connection between physical and emotional energy. Review the four types of energy on pages 59 – 68 in the book and identify one area that you want to strengthen in the next little while.
If your score = 12 & above	Excellent coaching begins with presence, which is fuelled by self-awareness and personal energy management. You see yourself frequently paying attention to the energy principles that contribute to a great conversation. Continue your great focus on this area, and perhaps ask for feedback as to how your "coachees" think that you could improve. Remember that on pages 59 – 68 in the book there may be some good ideas to help you continue to build your four kinds of energy.

Skill	Areas of Focus
Curious Questioning p. 69 - 81	• **Asking powerful questions** • **Uncovering different perspectives** • **Generating new and creative ideas**
If your score = 6 or below	Curiosity is a wonderful way to approach conversations and will set you up for discovering what you may not have known before. The concepts of powerful questions and uncovering perspectives may be particularly helpful for you. Refer to pages 69 – 81 in the book for specific practical ideas.
If your score = 7 to 11	Curiosity is a wonderful way to approach conversations and will set you up for discovering what you may not have known before. You are already using features of curiosity to assist in the coaching relationship. By focusing more on powerful questioning and listening to understand perspectives, you may find that the conversations become more robust. Remember too that silence is also an important part of the coaching process here. Refer to pages 69 – 81 in the book for other specific practical ideas.
If your score = 12 & above	Genuine curiosity makes the difference between your coachee feeling comfortable enough to share openly vs. feeling interrogated or judged. You are demonstrating a foundational strength to having great conversations so well done! Try having a 10 min conversation where you only use powerful questions and see what happens! Refer to page 69 – 81 in the book for other specific practical ideas.

Skill	Areas of Focus
Open Listening p. 83 - 100	• **Using open versus closed listening** • **Identifying deeply held values** • **Listening for feelings**
If your score = 6 or below	Open Listening is where the focus is clearly on the person that you are coaching, and you also have the opportunity to hear things that they haven't explicitly said. The aspect of listening for values and feelings can seem awkward to some, but they are a clue to what's important and currently happening for your coachee. Try slowing down to become more aware of what is happening in the moment. Refer to pages 83 – 100 for clues that will help you use these skills more frequently.
If your score = 7 to 11	Open Listening is where the focus is clearly on the person that you are coaching, and you may even hear things that they haven't explicitly said. With this score, you are being intentional about these aspects so state what you hear so that the coachee can verify the accuracy of your observations. Refer to pages 83 – 100 for clues that will help you use these skills more frequently.
If your score = 12 & above	Open Listening is where the focus is clearly on the person that you are coaching, and you may even hear things that they haven't explicitly said. You are clearly doing this with frequent attention, and probably uncovering ways to improve motivation and transparency. Refer to pages 83 – 100 as a helpful refresher, and perhaps you'll discover another skill to add to your approach.

Skill	Areas of Focus
Appreciative Discovery p. 101 - 108	• **Confirming talents & strengths** • **Creating new options for action** • **Generating excitement about positive possibilities**
If your score = 6 or below	Appreciative Discovery requires a fundamental shift to focus on talents and strengths and usually represents a different approach to coaching. Try focusing on this aspect to move away from a problem-centred approach to development. Perhaps try to find one opportunity a day to notice another's talents and strengths, and then say that to the person. Remember that there is information on pages 101- 108 in the book to help you move forward with this.
If your score = 7 to 11	Appreciative Discovery requires a fundamental shift to focus on talents and strengths and usually represents a different approach to coaching. You have begun to make this shift, and now it's time for you to apply your strengths to this opportunity! What do you do extremely well that helps you focus on this, and that you want to strengthen? Remember that there is information on pages 101 – 108 in the book that will help you sharpen this skill.
If your score = 12 & above	You understand that Appreciative Discovery requires a fundamental shift to focus on talents and strengths and this represents a different approach to coaching. Well done! Watch for continuing positivity to grow with increasing engagement, and continue to integrate the other skills that are also part of the trail map. Remember that there is information on pages 101 – 108 in the book that will continue to help you sharpen this skill.

Skill	Areas of Focus
Catalytic Feedback p. 109 - 125	• **Providing timely and realistic feedback** • **Championing successes** • **Celebrating capabilities**
If your score = 6 or below	Catalytic Feedback helps us learn from experience and when delivered with positive intent, it helps us grow. What is holding you back using feedback in a catalytic way? The word "feedback" tends to initially elicit negative responses so you will definitely enjoy pages 109 – 125 for a balanced approach to this topic.
If your score = 7 to 11	Catalytic Feedback helps us learn from experience and when delivered with positive intent, it helps us grow. Your frequency in this area is good, and remember that sometimes it's hard to measure impact of feedback. Perhaps you could get some feedback in this area to help you grow? Also remember that pages 109 – 125 help present a balanced approach to this topic.
If your score = 12 & above	Catalytic Feedback helps us learn from experience and when delivered with positive intent, it helps us grow. You are doing this with great frequency, and remember that sometimes it's hard to measure impact of that feedback. What are you noticing about the impact on those that you deliver feedback to? Remember that pages 109 – 125 help present a balanced approach to this topic.

Skill	Areas of Focus
Heightened Engagement p. 126 - 132	• **Targeting performance and results** • **Designing next steps** • **Reviewing progress**
If your score = 6 or below	Heightened Engagement is both an outcome and a set of skills that translates engagement into action, high performance and results. This is the area where the person's activities become aligned with the organization's goals and create positive results. Look closely at the area where you are not doing this, and perhaps see what mental shift (as outlined in Part II in the book) may be required. Pages 126 – 132 in the book will probably provide some clues for improvement here.
If your score = 7 to 11	Heightened Engagement is both an outcome and a set of skills that translates engagement into action, high performance and results. This is the area where the person's activities become aligned with the organization's goals and create positive results. You are doing this with some frequency, and you probably are seeing the positive results. Pages 126 – 132 in the book may provide a couple of additional ideas that can take you to the next level.
If your score = 12 & above	Heightened Engagement is both an outcome and a set of skills that translates engagement into action, high performance and results. This is the area where the person's activities become aligned with the organization's goals and create positive results. You are definitely making a difference to the individuals you coach as well as helping them create the results that are making a difference to their organization. Pages 126 – 132 in the book may provide a helpful review for you in this area.

Total Score	(out of 90)
75 – 90	Congratulations! It's clear that all of these areas contain demonstrated strengths for you and you are very diligent in applying coaching skills. It may be interesting for you to ask for some feedback from those you work with closely as to how your strengths are working for them, and also their suggested areas of development for you. You could also serve as an advocate within your organization for the power and impact of coaching. Let us know how we can help you move this forward.
60-75	You are on the right track and the coaching skills make sense to you. You are using them with some frequency, and the growth aspect for you may be practice and feedback. You are strongly contributing to your coachees' sense of achievement and personal value. The book "Coaching For Engagement" and the course "Coaching for Engagement" may be helpful resources for you to strengthen your already developed abilities.
45 to 60	The book "Coaching for Engagement" and the course "Coaching for Engagement" will help you move forward with your desire to integrate coaching skills into your leadership skills. You are already seeing glimpses of what can happen when you make the mental shifts that change how you are interacting with people. Congratulations on your progress to date!
Below 45	Congratulations, you've come across a possibility for self-development! The fact that you took this assessment indicates interest in this topic. The good news is that with the book "Coaching for Engagement", and the course "Coaching for Engagement", you will definitely increase your ability in these areas to develop and strengthen your coachees.

Acknowledgements

Every book owes a debt of gratitude to a wide array of people both past and present. Yet some people were especially important to its development – planting the seeds, or coming to our aid at critical moments in the process. For that we will always be grateful.

The seeds for this book sprouted out of one of Tekara's leadership development programs for managers called Coaching Conversations, which later became Coaching for Engagement™. The program began as a project to identify common themes from the professional coaching world, and to make them relevant for managers and leaders. The first iteration was pulled together by Cresswell Walker. The second version, with the new COACH acronym, was the product of Dr. Brian Fraser, Dave Koot and Bob Hancox. We spent many hours reviewing, debating and revising how to make the model relevant and memorable. In the process, we learned a lot about utilizing each other's strengths. Marion McAdam was also involved in creating the current format of the 2-day Coaching for Engagement™ workshop, and assisted with business development. We are deeply indebted to all of them for their thought leadership, professionalism, friendship, and warm support.

Our heartfelt thanks also go out to our colleagues in the Tekara community including: Barry Billings, Isabelle Clements, Tom Dent, Annabelle Donovan, Leona Kolla, Laurie MacDonald, Phyllis Macintyre, Claire Simpkins, Neil Chin Aleong, and Shoshana Alice. We are blessed to work with such a brilliant, caring, and authentic group of people who've been a big part of our development personally and professionally over the years. Their support and input as this book took shape provided us with the necessary energy and insight to keep moving forward. Special thanks to Leona for reviewing the first draft, and providing sage advice that shaped a much improved manuscript. Special thanks also to Neil and Peter for reviewing the final draft.

Elizabeth Miller's diligent copy editing of the final manuscript is gratefully acknowledged.

Thank you to the hundreds of clients we've been fortunate enough to serve. The work of organizational development requires resilience, a deep belief in the potential of people, and a sense of adventure. We've seen these qualities time and time again, and learned from every leader and organizations we've had the privilege of working with. We're inspired by the passion they bring to changing the energy and impact of business.

Bob Hancox

One of the things that I have loved about coaching from the very beginning is dropping the illusion that you need to have all of the answers – especially about where you get in life.

My work life, friends and family have become intertwined over the years. My relationships with some of the people closest to me started off in a work context. Certainly this is true for Peter Lee, the "soul of Tekara" and the person who initially challenged me to look at coaching as a profession. Peter has always been able to see future trends around the corner and has encouraged me to fully live my calling and profession. We've been friends and colleagues for almost 20 years now and I acknowledge the profound influence he has had on my working life. Without his guidance and leadership, this book would never have been completed.

I have learned so much from my clients and friends over the years that when it came to writing the book, I knew I needed to hear from them. I interviewed & talked to Bart, Brian, Carollyne, Cress, Dale, Dan, Dave, Dave W, Eeva, Gail, Howie, James, Judith, Kajal, Ken, Kim, Lawell, Linda S, Mark F, Martin, Nettie, Paul, Peter, Rachna S, Rob, Russ W, Ravi, Sanjay, Scott, Shelly, Thomas, Tim, Dr. Tom, Walter, Weiliang and Yvonne who all shared great insights that shaped the texture of the book. I know you always miss someone on a list and I ask for your forgiveness in advance if I missed you.

Crystal Ironside, my invaluable Executive Assistant, amazes me with her ability to organize and implement complex tasks. Her enthusiastic support on this project, in addition to many aspects of my professional world, enabled me to accomplish more than I thought possible this year.

I also want to acknowledge my own coach, Lydia Richards, for role modeling great coaching, integrated into a life of service and faith.

There's no question that my wife Adrienne has provided long-standing love and support for me in this process and I'm very thankful for her belief in me as I pursue my calling. My daughters – Christie and Julia have endured my practice coaching and I eventually learned to ask them "What would you like me to do - coach you, listen to you or give you advice?" Over the years, they ask for advice less and less often, preferring coaching and listening.

My parents first modeled for me the value of great conversations. I am deeply indebted to them, and to my brothers, Bill and Bruce, who helped me finally realize that we didn't always have to fight to get to understanding!

I want to thank my co-author Russ for his continually positive attitude to working together in many areas over the years. He is one of the most dedicated and positive people that I know and I admire his ability to set great goals and go for them. He has done that consistently in his life whether it's doing triathlons, starting a foundation, or leading Tekara's Energy for Performance™ work. Thanks, Russ for partnering with me on this coaching journey.

There is no question that this book would not have evolved into the final product without my other co-author Kristann's expertise and thoughtful, professional contribution and I am extremely grateful for her involvement.

Finally, God has always been in control. As a result I am very thankful for the past and present, while looking forward with hope to the future.

Russell Hunter

When we embarked on this project I underestimated how transformative the process of writing a book would be. It provided me with the opportunity to meet and work with some amazing individuals and organizations, challenge my assumptions, and explore new ways of working and living. I will never be the same as a result.

My personal philosophy and approach to coaching, engagement, leadership development and change management was catalyzed by the works of several provocative thought leaders - most notably; John Whitmore, Robert Kegan, Thomas Crane, Jim Loehr, Robert Hargrove, Chip and Dan Heath, Daniel Pink, Susan Scott, David Rock, Tim Gallwey, Robert Cooper, John Kotter, Marcus Bucking ham, Peter Block, Peter Senge and John Eliot.

Our colleagues at Tekara provided a regular dose of grounded optimism and faith in what we could bring to managers worldwide through this book. Peter was especially helpful to both the inception and ultimate delivery of the final product. He helped us get through key sticking points along the way, whether creative, financial, or emotional, to ensure we kept our vision for this project alive.

The passion of Dr. Jim Loehr, Chris Osorio, Chris Allredge, and the team at the Human Performance Institute continues to inspire me. My understanding of energy management, as it applies to coaching for engagement, would not be complete without their continued focus and resilience.

My "sixwigs" team at Royal Roads University provided the perfect blend of support, challenge, and fun in taking my coaching skills and presence to a new level. Enduring friendships with Anna Lisa, Kelly, Janice, Larry and John continue to be a refuge when the pace of work and life grow turbulent.

Bob brings a level of authenticity and heart to everything he invests in; I've admired that in him since the first day we met. He taught me by example that great coaching isn't just something you do as a leader – it's a mindset that reflects who you are. His ability to inspire trust, provoke amazing conversations, and believe in people more than they often believe in themselves, made him an invaluable partner and collaborator.

Kristann's multi-faceted set of skills and perspective added a degree of rigour necessary to move our writing to the next level. Her resilience despite an ever shifting set of demands and responsibilities inspired me to find gratitude and presence when the writing got tough.

The support of my family created clarity when I needed it most. My wife Vivienne not only supported me with her words of encouragement, but protected the space and time necessary for me to create and write, often at the expense of her own. On a daily basis my young daughter and son remind me that one of our great capacities as human beings is one we often neglect in adulthood – a profound sense of curiosity. And my parents have supported me no matter what I managed to get myself into since birth. They taught me that great coaching isn't only about what you say, but often about what you don't say.

Kristann Boudreau

I'm grateful to my co-authors, Bob and Russ, for bringing a collaborative spirit to the project, for "walking the talk" and using the core coaching skills in our working conversations, and for trusting me to honour their original vision for the book in my writing. My thanks to Peter Lee at Tekara for making my involvement in this project possible, and for his continuous urging and reminder to "keep it practical." On the home front, I would like to acknowledge my husband, Chris, for his moral support, encouragement, and listening ear at the end of a long day of writing; and for spending extra time with our son during the intensive final stages of writing.

About the Authors

Bob Hancox

For over 25 years Bob has been a successful leader in public and private sector organizations - specializing in leadership coaching and organizational development. His life's mission is to strengthen leaders by designing and implementing programs and approaches that help people develop their authentic leadership abilities.

As the lead of the Strategic Coaching Practice for Tekara, Bob is a Certified Professional Co-Active Coach (CPCC) with thousands of hours of coaching hundreds of leaders. His coaching clients include Board Directors, CEO's and senior leaders across Canada, the United States, Europe, China and India. Bob is also a key developer of Tekara's Coaching for Engagement™ program and has delivered that program in Canada, India and China. Bob was selected as one of three finalists for the prestigious 2009 Coaches Canada Canadian Coach of the Year Award.

Russell Hunter

Russ is the National Director of the Human Performance Institute Canada and an associate consultant with Tekara Organizational Effectiveness. He brings over 15 years of experience as a business leader, keynote speaker, facilitator, and Certified Executive Coach (CEC).

As a former CEO of Boldeye Solutions (an integrated marketing consulting firm) Russ worked with hundreds of business leaders and managers worldwide to create breakthrough performance. He has contributed articles on engagement to leading publications including; The Wall Street Journal, Fortune, and Canadian Business. He speaks frequently on the topics of leadership, energy management, cultivating high performance and engagement at business conferences and events worldwide. As an accomplished Ironman triathlete, Russ continues to love training and competing in races across North America and Europe.

Kristann Boudreau

Kristann focuses primarily on designing powerful learning experiences and programs in the areas of leadership development and personal effectiveness. She brings both experience and training as a group facilitator, adult educator and professional coach. Kristann uses her research skills to keep current with the thinking of key authors in business, and to hunt for new tools, models and best practices for Tekara to apply in our work with clients.

Before joining Tekara, she spent several years working in the field of environmental management and stakeholder engagement in a large corporation. During that time, Kristann experienced first-hand the challenges facing young professionals and emerging leaders today. She is passionate about equipping leaders at all levels with the skills and tools to create workplaces where every individual is known and valued for their unique contribution.

About Tekara Organizational Effectiveness

Amazing Conversations - Strategic Leadership - Extraordinary Results

Founded in 1994, Tekara Organizational Effectiveness is a leadership and organizational development consulting firm based in Vancouver, Canada.

We work side by side with leaders and managers to help them achieve extraordinary performance and results at individual, team and organizational levels. A key characteristic that distinguishes Tekara is our commitment to supporting individuals and teams to speak openly and honestly to one another. Our strength lies in helping leaders engage in candid conversation and real dialogue, paving the way for more productive working relationships and more cohesive teams, which in turn, generate the performance and results that our clients strive to achieve.

Our work focuses on five critical and interconnected factors that drive business success: leadership, strategy, culture, structure, and execution. Coaching plays a key role in our business: we provide leadership coaching, we provide coaching skills training through our Coaching for Engagement™ Program, and, whenever we are consulting for clients on organizational issues, we use coaching to help build their capacity to tackle the challenge they hired us to address, leaving them better equipped next time around.

Our clients include hundreds of private and public sector organizations located throughout Canada, the United States, Europe and Asia.

For additional information on Tekara, please visit: **www.tekara.com**

ORGANIZATIONAL EFFECTIVENESS INC.

Tekara's Coaching for Engagement™ Program

In today's workplace, coaching skills are essential for leaders and managers to engage employees, heighten their performance, and help them produce sustainable results. Based on the concepts explored in this book, the Coaching for Engagement™ Program is a practical learning experience designed to develop the core mindset and key coaching skills used by successful managers worldwide.

Participants learn:

- Why coaching conversations are essential for today's leaders
- How coaching conversations connect to bottom-line results
- When to have coaching conversations (and when not to)
- How to offer timely, responsive, and powerful feedback
- The role of trust and transformation in coaching conversations
- Five guidelines for developing enhanced listening skills;
- What to do when employees resists coaching conversations.

Unlike most learning experiences which finish at the end of the classroom session, Coaching for Engagement™ provides each participant with follow-up coaching once they have had a chance to practice the skills in their own working relationships. This ensures each participant gets the support they need to build confidence and put their skills into practice, rather than just learning the concepts.

The Coaching for Engagement™ Program can also be tailored to suit your specific schedule constraints.

For additional information on how to bring Coaching for Engagement™ into your organization, please visit: **www.tekara.com**

Endnotes

---

[1] Gidget Hopf, quoted in *"Leading with Questions: How Leaders Find the Right Solutions By Knowing What to Ask"* by Michael Marquardt (Jossey-Bass, 2005). Pages 118-119.

[2] If you have an interest in learning more about some of the latest research on the surprisingly powerful intrinsic motivators for employees (versus extrinsic motivators like the "carrot" of performance bonuses and the "stick" of being criticized or demoted), check out Daniel Pink's latest book *"Drive: The Surprising Truth About What Motivates Us"* (Riverhead, 2009). To view a 10-minute video clip summarizing his thinking, visit: http://www.youtube.com/watch?v=u6XAPnuFjJc. For a slightly lengthier 20-minute video clip, visit: http://www.youtube.com/watch?v=rrkrvAUbU9Y&feature=sdig&et=1251728132.58.

[3] Figure adapted from *"Quiet Leadership: Six Steps to Transforming Performance at Work"* by David Rock (Collins Business, 2006). Page 39.

[4] *"Primal Leadership: Realizing the Power of Emotional Intelligence"* by Daniel Goleman, Richard Boyatzis and Annie McKee (Harvard Business Press, 2002). See the section entitled *"Leadership Styles in Nutshell"* in Chapter 4 *"The Leadership Repertoire."*

[5] Same as previous.

[6] Both Towers Perrin and The Gallup Organization are leading researchers in levels of employee engagement globally. Towers Perrin's most recent publicly available research in their *"2007-2008 Towers Perrin Global Workforce Study."* For an overview of the key findings, visit: http://www.towersperrin.com/tp/getwebcachedoc?webc=HRS/USA/2008/200802/GWS_handout_web.pdf. Some of The Gallup Organization's most recent findings about employee engagement levels in the United States are presented in online article entitled *"Despite the Downturn, Employees Remain Engaged"* by Jennifer Robison (January 14, 2010) available at: http://gmj.gallup.com/content/125036/despite-downturn-employees-remain-engaged.aspx#1.

[7] *"Generation Y: What Millenial Workers Want: How to Attract and Retain Gen Y Employees"* by Robert Half International (2008). Available for download at: www.theiia.org/download.cfm?file=67170.

[8] The ideas outlined in the table are influenced by two sources. The first is a section entitled "When to Coach and When Not to Coach" in the book "A Manager's Guide to Coaching: Simple and Effective Ways to Get the Best Out of Your Employees" by Brian Emerson and Anne Loehr (AMACOM, 20008). The second is a section entitled "Barriers to Coaching: What does Coachability Look Like" in the book "The Coaching Manager: Developing Top Talent in Business" by James M. Hunt and Joseph R. Weintraub (Sage Publications Inc., 2002).

[9] *"The Self-Fulfilling Prophecy"* by Cliff Grimes (Accel Team, 2009). Accessed online in June 2010 at: http://www.accel-team.com/pygmalion/atPDF_11_Pygmalion_np.pdf

[10] "Speed Lead: Faster, Simpler ways to Manage People, Projects and Teams in Complex Companies" by Kevan Hall (Nicholas Brealey Publishing, 2006). Page 136.

[11] For an introduction to the Johari Window tool in its original form, visit Wikipedia (a free online encyclopedia) at: http://en.wikipedia.org/wiki/Johari_window

[12] "Coaching to Solutions: A Manager's Toolkit for Performance Delivery" by Carole Pemberton (Butterworth-Heineman, 2006). See Chapter 4, "Putting the principles into practice: You don't have to understand the cause of a problem to solve it."

[13] "Some psychologists practice a school of behavior therapy that encourages the client to "act as if" a certain state is true, no matter how unreasonable it seems. We change behavior, says this school, not be delving into the past or by trying to align motives with actions but rather by "acting as if" the change

should happen. It's much easier to act your way into feelings than to feel your way into actions." Source: "Grace Notes" by Philip Yancey (Zondervan, 2009).

[14] All of the content in this chapter discussing the concepts of energy and energy management are based on the book "*The Power of Full Engagement: Managing Energy, Not Time, is the Key to High Performance and Personal Renewal*" by Jim Loehr and Tony Schwartz (Free Press, 2003)

[15] Adapted from the book "*The Power of Full Engagement: Managing Energy, Not Time, is the Key to High Performance and Personal Renewal*" by Jim Loehr and Tony Schwartz (Free Press, 2003). Page 38.

[16] This client asked to remain anonymous. Personal communication: Summer 2009.

[17] "Coaching to Solutions: A Manager's Toolkit for Performance Delivery" by Carole Pemberton (Butterworth-Heineman, 2006). See Chapter 1, "How Much Time?"

[18] "*Einstein and the Poet*" by William Hermanns (Branden Press, 1983). Page 147.

[19] Alex Osborn, a pioneer in facilitating creativity, developed this list of "idea-spurring questions." They were later arranged by Bob Eberle as the mnemonic S.C.A.M.P.E.R.

[20] Josh McDaniels, Coach of the Denver Broncos of the National Football League. Quoted in "*Tim Tebow: The Making of a Quaterback*" by Peter King (Sports Illustrated, June 14 2010). Pages 63-64. Also accessible online at: http://sportsillustrated.cnn.com/vault/article/magazine/MAG1170592/2/index.htm.

[21] Gail Pickard. Personal communication: Summer 2009.

[22] Weiliang Le, Managing Director, Shanghai Development Center, SAP Business Objects. Personal communication: Summer 2009.

[23] Chinese Business Review, May 2007

[24] Thomas Guerrero, Director, Patient Care Quality Review Boards Secretariat, British Columbia Ministry of Health. Personal communication: Summer 2009.

[25] "*Building Conflict Competent Teams*" by Craig E. Runde and Tim A. Flanagan (John Wiley & Sons Inc., 2008), pages 96-100.

[26] In the mid-eighties, David Cooperrider and his associates at Case Western Reserve University introduced the term Appreciative Inquiry. David's artist wife Nancy brought the "appreciative eye" perspective to David's attention. The idea of the appreciative eye assumes that in every piece of art there is beauty. Art is a beautiful idea translated into a concrete form. Cooperrider applied the notion to business: to the appreciative eye, organizations are expressions of beauty and spirit, ideas translated into action. To learn more, read "*Appreciative Inquiry: A Positive Revolution in Change*" by David L. Cooperrider and Diana Whitney (Berrett-Koehler Publishder, 2005). You can also visit: http://appreciativeinquiry.case.edu.

[27] "*Strengths Finder 2.0*" by Tom Rath (Gallup Press, 2007). Page iii.

[28] "*Strengths Finder 2.0*" by Tom Rath (Gallup Press, 2007). Page iv.

[29] "Strengths Based Leadership: Great Leaders, Teams and Why People Follow" by Tom Rath and Barry Conchie (Gallup Press, 2008), Page 14.

[30] Cited as an example in a video clip of Daniel Pink summarizing his book "*Drive: The Surprising Truth About What Motivates Us*" (produced by RSA Animate). Accessed at http://www.youtube.com/watch?v=u6XAPnuFjJc on June 24, 2010.

[31] Rob Eisses, former CEO of Icron. Personal communication: Summer 2009.

[32] *"The Feedback Sandwich is Out to Lunch"* by Shelle Rose Charvet. Accessible online at: http://www.successstrategies.com/news-and-media/articles-interviews/Feedback_sandwich.php

[33] *"Coaching for Improved Work Performance"* by Ferdinand Fournies. (McGraw-Hill, 2000). Pages 101-102.

[34] "Coaching to Solutions: A Manager's Toolkit for Performance Delivery" by Carole Pemberton (Butterworth-Heineman, 2006). See Chapter 8, "Reality Bites: Expanding Reality Through Feedback."

[35] Mathematical modeling of positive to negative ratios by Barbara Frederickson and Marcel Losada. Cited in *"How Full Is Your Bucket?"* by Tom Rath and Donald O. Clifton (Gallup Press, 2004).

[36] These questions are drawn from two sources. The first is *"Searching for Exceptions"* in Chapter 8 of *"Coaching to Solutions: A Manager's Toolkit for Performance Delivery"* by Carole Pemberton (Butterworth-Heineman, 2006). The second is *"When does the solution – or part of it – happen already?"* in Chapter 5 of *"The Solutions Focus: Making Coaching and Change SIMPLE"* (Nicholas Brealey Publishing, 2007, 2nd edition).

[37] Claire Simpkins, Associate, Tekara Organizational Effectiveness. Personal communication (Summer, 2009).

[38] "To the Vulnerable Go the Spoils: New evidence indicates that our ability to "click" with colleagues can make or break a career" by Ori Brafman and Rom Brafman (Bloomberg Businessweek, June 14-20, 2010). Pages 71-73..

[39] Linda Sartorio. Personal communication: Summer 2009.

[40] See footnote 36.

[41] Sanjay Dutt, CEO of RvaluE Learning Systems (our Coaching Conversations™ partner in India). Personal communication: Summer 2009.

[42] Mark Frezell, Director of Inflight, WestJet. Personal communication: Summer 2009.

[43] *"Try Feedforward Instead of Feedback"* by Marshall Goldsmith. Accessed at: http://marshallgoldsmithlibrary.com/docs/articles/Feedforward.doc

[44] According to Wikipedia (http://en.wikipedia.org/wiki/Four_stages_of_competence), the "Four Stages of Learning" or "Conscious Competence Theory" originated with Abraham Maslow. US Gordon Training International organization played a role in defining and promoting the conscious competence theory as part of their teacher effectiveness training programs in the early 1970's. Since that time, it is referred to widely and commonly. For more information, also see: http://www.businessballs.com/consciouscompetencelearningmodel.htm#origins

[45] This four-stage development process is based on the three-stage development process described in *"The Power of Full Engagement: Managing Energy, Not Time, is the Key to High Performance and Personal Renewal"* by Dr. Jim Loehr and Tony Schwartz (Free Press, 2003).

[46] *"The Power of Full Engagement: Managing Energy, Not Time, Is the Key to High Performance"* by Dr. Jim Loehr and Tony Schwartz (Free Press, 2003). Page 166.

[47] Personal communication: Summer 2009.